Medicine and Society

HENRY MILLER

OXFORD UNIVERSITY PRESS 1973

Oxford University Press, *Ely House, London W.1.*

Glasgow	Delhi
New York	Bombay
Toronto	Calcutta
Melbourne	Madras
Wellington	Karachi
Cape Town	Lahore
Ibadan	Dacca
Nairobi	Kuala Lumpur
Dar es Salaam	Singapore
Lusaka	Hong Kong
Addis Ababa	Tokyo

CASEBOUND ISBN 0 19 858321 4
PAPERBACK ISBN 0 19 858322 2

Typesetting by
Linocomp Ltd., Marcham, Berkshire
Printed in Great Britain by
J. W. Arrowsmith Ltd., Bristol, England

'Medicine is a social science and politics nothing else but medicine on a large scale'

RUDOLF VIRCHOW
(1821–1902)

Preface

This book is concerned with the impact of the revolution in bio-medical science on society and on current medical practice. It deals with the present state of medicine in the advanced countries, the historical background of present developments, and some possibilities for the future. The social implications of present and impending advance comprise the insatiable demands of the health services for new resources of money and personnel; issues of priority within the service; and new ethical problems raised by our increasing ability to alter the course of many serious illnesses, to extend the span of life, and to control population. The mood of introspective concern that characterizes medicine today was perhaps immediately excited by the dramatic debut of heart transplantation, with its emphasis on the contrast beween 'big' and 'little' medicine, and on possible areas of conflict between the needs of the individual and those of society. No doubt forebodings about the possibility of genetic manipulation also played a part. But the difficulties of the situation are really of longer standing.

Medicine has changed more in the last forty years than in the previous four hundred. However, the political problems contingent on this change have yet to be faced. They are too important to be left to the necessarily empirical judgement of the medical profession. The aim of this book is to contribute to the dialogue that is a necessary prelude to inescapable decisions of public policy.

Newcastle upon Tyne　　　　　　　　　　　　　　　　H.M.
January 1973

Contents

The scientific revolution in medicine

We owe the increase in the population of Britain that began in the eighteenth century to a falling death-rate rather than to a rising birth-rate, and it began before medicine was sufficiently developed to have any material effect on either parameter. The even more rapid acceleration in population growth that characterized the nineteenth century also owed little to the medical profession. It was due in the main to the improved standards of living that came with the industrial revolution, and particularly to the increasing control of communicable diseases by sanitation. Ironically, the infant's chances of survival were better in the squalid streets that surrounded the mills and factories of the 1850s than in the supposedly arcadian environment of the subsistence agriculture that yielded recruits for the new industries. The striking decline in the incidence of tuberculosis during the middle years of the nineteenth century, for example, was almost certainly related to improved nutritional standards. The only specific contribution of medicine to this process was the widespread employment of vaccination against smallpox after 1800, an empirical technique that long preceded the faintest glimmerings of knowledge about immunology. Cholera was similarly brought under fairly effective control by hygienic measures years before the causal organism was recognized by Koch in 1883, and even before the germ theory of infectious disease was formulated by Pasteur in the 1860s.

The impact of the scientific revolution in medicine on public as opposed to personal health is not yet clear, except for its evident influence on the age-distribution of the population, and the chances are that its operation will become fully evident in vital statistics only in the later years of the present century. Modern medicine can reasonably be said to have begun with the *Cellular pathology* (*Cellularpathologie*) of Rudolf Virchow published in 1858. For a time at the turn of the century the discovery of hormones and vitamins suggested that the physiology laboratories of the universities would hold the lead in new developments in medicine and therapeutics. But it was not long before chemistry asserted its supremacy as a source of medical advance, and the genius of the chemist in synthesizing vitamins and hormones themselves has gradually reduced our dependence even on these natural biological products. Almost the only exceptions are the extraction of parathyroid hormone from the products of the slaughterhouse and of growth hormone from human pituitary glands removed at post-mortem. Indeed the scientific revolution in medical treatment began with Paul Ehrlich's introduction of the 'magic bullet' Salvarsan for the treatment of syphilis in 1910. Ehrlich was the father of chemotherapy and the first worker deliberately to use the methods of scientific biochemistry to devise methods of killing the causal agents of disease without deleterious effect on the patient's tissues.

The next great step forward came with the development of the sulphonamide drugs almost simultaneously in France and Britain in the 1930s. Unlike Salvarsan, these drugs had a wide range of effectiveness and removed the fear and horror of bacterial sepsis from childbirth, severe physical injury, and surgical operation. They also turned pneumococcal pneumonia from a frequently fatal illness into one that could be cured within a few days by a handful of tablets—and in doing so caused chaos in medicine in the United States, which had just embarked on a massive and elaborate scheme for the production of anti-pneumococcal serum on a national scale.

Prior to these developments, medical treatment had been largely symptomatic. Opium, quinine, and digitalis had of course been known for many years, but all the innovations came from the chemical industry, together with techniques for purifying and standardizing drugs and for establishing reliable methods of measuring their activity and efficacy. Aspirin had been introduced in 1899 and curiously enough remains the most effective of the minor analgesics, as well as the best and safest anti-rheumatic remedy. Veronal was the first barbiturate to be successfully used in medicine in 1903, and phenobarbitone (Bayer's 'Luminal'), introduced in 1912, is still the most widely used drug in the treatment of epilepsy. These were the first of an extensive range of barbiturate drugs that remain invaluable in the treatment of sleeplessness, anxiety, and agitation.

However, these drugs are for the control of symptoms rather than the treatment of causes.

The sophisticated march of chemotherapy continues, with the introduction of Septrin (Bactrim) in 1968 for a broad range of bacterial diseases. The production of penicillin early in the Second World War opened up a new era, and streptomycin, tetracycline, and the more sophisticated modern antibiotics (especially the synthetic penicillins) have virtually completed the conquest not only of bacterial infection but also of spirochaetal diseases including syphilis. So far, at any rate, pharmacology has kept ahead of the increasing number of organisms that have acquired resistance to antibiotics. Significantly the virus, intimately embodied in the protoplasm of the patient's cells, is less accessible, and the triumphs of clinical virology (the conquest of poliomyelitis especially) have been prophylactic and preventive rather than therapeutic. The most recent chapter in this story comprises the development of effective protection against measles, rubella (German measles), and mumps. Although these are banal diseases their incidence is enormous and they exact a considerable social toll in the form of complications which are sometimes serious, and through the interruption of education.

One branch of medicine which has made enormous strides in the last two decades is anaesthesia, and it is no exaggeration to state that modern surgery is possible only because of modern anaesthesia, which renders prolonged and complicated operations both safer for the patient and very much less difficult for the surgeon. Intensive care and the maintenance of the unconscious patient are to a considerable extent by-products of anaesthesiology, since the anaesthetist is expert in the maintenance of assisted respiration and this is the essential technique of intensive care. Before the war the head-injured patient was largely left to nature. He was fortunate to survive several days' unconsciousness, for nursing skills, especially in the maintenance of adequate pulmonary ventilation, were undeveloped, and little or nothing was known of the biochemical changes secondary to prolonged coma. We know that intensive care also yields valuable dividends in useful survival in many other cases of prolonged unconsciousness such as that due to poisoning; in respiratory paralysis of neurological origin, which is often recoverable; and in tetanus. Intensive care for coronary disease is a different and more problematical issue. The wiring up of a patient with coronary thrombosis to his elaborate instrumentation is a pleasing exercise in technical virtuosity, but evidence of the superiority of the treatment of cardiac infarction, in which the blood supply to a portion of heart muscle is cut off by coronary artery thrombosis, in an intensive coronary care unit over its simple management at home is not entirely convincing; in fact the only controlled trial so far published even hints that the opposite may be the case.

The conquest of most of the acute and chronic infections in the developed world has left medicine now preoccupied with a large number of diseases of multiple aetiology and long duration, where the assessment of therapeutic results presents real difficulties. The success of penicillin in treating pneumonia or syphilis was so dramatic and so unequivocal that it required little in the way of controlled therapeutic trial, but this does not apply to many of the chronic conditions now under discussion, where carefully planned prospective long-term studies are absolutely essential for the evaluation of any form of treatment. However there is one field in which the patient's life can almost certainly be saved from a chronic disease which was invariably fatal ten years ago. This is chronic renal failure. The 'artificial kidney', which filters out toxic impurities from the patient's blood by dialysis, was originally introduced for the treatment of acute reversible renal failure, such as that induced by surgical shock or poisoning causing damage to the tubules of the kidney. Here dialysis often sustains life until spontaneous recovery ensues. However, the results of such treatment were so dramatically successful that its employment was soon extended to succour the victim of chronic kidney disease of other types, poisoned by the accumulation of urea and other toxic metabolites in the blood. It soon became evident that in many cases life could be maintained almost indefinitely by regular dialysis, and a little later that kidney transplantation at an appropriate time could often yield a functioning kidney and allow twice-weekly dialysis to be discontinued. This is truly life-saving medicine, practised in a situation that was previously entirely inaccessible to treatment. The problems that have arisen in the demand for resources occasioned by this remarkably successful form of therapy are discussed below.

There have been many other striking advances in clinical pharmacology, but there are two especially that benefit a sufficient number of patients to deserve special mention. Within the last decade the treatment of severely raised blood pressure has been improved out of recognition by the development of a series of drugs of increasing efficacy and decreasing toxicity that block the pathways in the sympathetic nervous system that play an essential part in the rise of arterial pressure. These drugs have completely altered the outlook for many patients with severe vascular hypertension, and over the years they are bound to exert a significant influence in delaying or averting the cardiac failure and cerebral haemorrhage that usually kill the subjects of severe hypertension.

The development of psychopharmacology has been even more remarkable. Its benefits are not reflected in tables of mortality, but in the increased happiness and social effectiveness of a very large number of patients. The history of these drugs is well-known. The first that were used deliberately to influence mood were the amphetamines, but their action is too brief to make them truly effective therapeutic agents. The use of monoamine oxidase inhibitors (or MAO drugs) arose, as is often the case in medicine, from the chance observation that certain patients treated for tuberculosis with a drug of this group showed a remarkable elevation of mood. These drugs were then found to influence a proportion of severely depresed patients even when no evident physical disease was present. Increasingly the MAO drugs have been replaced by the tricyclic antidepressants of the imipramine group which in turn have been modified and improved. This is probably the most important development in medical treatment since the discovery of penicillin. It has transformed the outlook for many patients severely crippled by recurrent depressive illness and obsessional states, and has gradually reduced the need for electroconvulsive therapy and hospital admission. The change from a state of retarded and suicidal depression to virtual normality within a few weeks is one of the most dramatic phenomena in clinical medicine, and it occurs often enough to have been confirmed by controlled clinical trial. It has also evoked a tentative hypothesis of depressive illness as a manifestation of disturbed metabolism of catecholamines in the basal parts of the brain, especially noradrenalin, which is known to be involved in the conduction of nerve impulses. This hypothesis has considerable implications for future psychiatric thinking. The treatment of schizophrenia has so far been less dramatically successful, but in selected cases drugs of the phenothiazine group have met with considerable success. Many patients for example with florid and paranoid syndromes have been able to return to the community in a fairly normal and effective condition, who would otherwise have had to be detained in hospital over long periods for their own and society's protection. It will be noted that these advances in psychiatry have been pharmacological and unconnected with the psychopathological concepts that continue to dominate popular thinking in this field. The results of the modern treatment of mental illness with drugs confirm the greater importance of disturbed biochemistry than of psychological factors in the causation of serious mental illness, and there can be little doubt that this represents one of the most important growing points of clinical research during the next few decades.

Drug problems

There are two by-products of the contemporary revolution in pharmacology that particularly excite present concern—first the volume of iatrogenic disease that results directly or indirectly from medical treatment, and secondly the increasing use of drugs for non-medical purposes.

In relation to the first of these it is above all necessary to preserve a sense of proportion. It is true, for example, that carbamazepine (Tegretol) produces bone-marrow depression that causes a fatal blood disease in something like one in ten thousand patients treated for the intolerable agony of trigeminal neuralgia, that such an idiosyncratic occasional outcome is entirely unpredictable—and when it occurs it is likely to be widely publicized. What is not made clear to the public is that no neurosurgeon would claim an operative mortality anything like as low as one in ten thousand for the same condition; however, we have not yet been conditioned to accept the rare fatality of medical treatment with the equanimity that attaches to the commoner disasters of surgery. Today's physicians must steel themselves to affirm in coroners' courts that treatment with effective modern drugs very often implies a small calculated risk of more or less serious side-effects—and that the risk is consciously and tacitly accepted because it is enormously outweighed by the much greater chance that the drug will restore health or actually save life. However, the complications of modern medical treatment certainly loom large in textbooks of therapeutics, and occupy a sizeable fraction of beds in any medical ward. They account, for example, for about one in twenty of all acute medical admissions, and for one-third of all dermatological consultations requested in a general hospital: there is scarcely a drug that has not been known to produce an occasional skin rash, and the result may vary from a transient blush to complete shedding of the skin with severe toxic illness. Antibiotics, drugs of the cortisone groups, and contraceptive pills are prone to lead to fungus infections of mouth, vagina, or gullet. The complications of treatment with cortisone and its analogues comprise a veritable textbook of medicine—water retention, raised blood-pressure, gastro-intestinal bleeding, fractures due to demineralization of the skeleton, muscle disease, and madness are but a few of the more dramatic. The antidepressive drugs may not only induce mania but also retention of urine, and glaucoma with a dangerous rise of intra-ocular pressure. Indeed the gamut of iatrogenic disease ranges from the banal effect of sustained digitalis overdosage so common in the elderly patient with cardiac disease, to the esoteric but unquestionable increase in the incidence of cancer caused by long-term immuno-suppressive treatment in patients rescued from certain death by renal transplantation.

This is a blood-curdling account, but it is well to bear in mind first that most of these complications can be prevented, that they are usually easily recognizable, and that in all but a few instances they can either be rapidly reversed by withdrawal of the drug, or successfully treated. When they are set against the phenomenal benefits we continue to derive from the current explosion in pharmacological knowledge and technique—and I refer to the relief of pain, disablement, and distress rather than to mere prolongation of life, which is not always an indubitable benefit—they can reasonably be regarded as not much more than an inconvenient nuisance.

The non-medical use of drugs is a highly topical subject, and apocalyptic forecasts of impending social disaster on this account are the stock-in-trade of parliamentarians and self-appointed guardians of public morality. In this connection a sense of historical perspective is essential but rarely manifest. It emphasizes the powerful combination of extreme irrationality and passionate indignation that invests the whole subject, the role of social and cultural factors rather than of either pharmacology or individual personality deviations in determining the pattern of drug usage, and of course the influence of example and often quite evanescent fashion. The 80 per cent of American soldiers in Vietnam who used cannabis and the 15 per cent who became regular users were very little different from their coevals at home, but they found themselves through no fault of their own in a catastrophically different social situation.

The very use of the term 'drug' is emotive and begs the question. Alcohol and tobacco are by far the most important and most dangerous drugs used in the western world, but they are not what the journalist has in mind when he discusses the problems of drug addicts. The employment of psycho-active substances is as old as recorded history, and there is no time or place when they have not been employed or where some have not been arbitrarily regarded as entirely acceptable, and the use of others as criminal. In the nineteenth century opium in one form or another was very widely used in Britain, especially by the poor and miserable, and contemporary medical literature extolled its superiority to alcohol in its effect on behaviour. The same view was supported by Indian rulers who strongly resisted the introduction of spirits into their territories in favour of the retention of the opium habit. Much the same applies to cannabis; the Indian Hemp Commission of 1894 commented on the rarity of serious ill-effects, their limitation to the users of the drug, and the lack of any serious impact on society. On the other hand the use of cannabis in the United States still puts the user at risk of a 40-year prison sentence, while in other countries and at other times both the sale of opium and the use of tobacco have been capital offences. It is notoriously easy to forgive one's own vices and be censorious about those of others, but in this instance the attitudes of our society can only be regarded as breathtaking. There are about 7000 convictions for the possession of cannabis annually and less than 300 heroin addicts in Britain, where the smoking of 350 million cigarettes a day (at an annual profit to the revenue of over £1000 million) causes more than 40 000 deaths and contributes at the very least to another 150 000 annually. We have more than 350 000 chronic alcoholics, with a suicide rate eighty times the normal; the best available evidence indicates that alcohol plays some part in at least two-thirds of all the crime committed in the country, and is directly associated with a higher proportion of crimes of violence from football hooliganism to murder. We spend millions of pounds on advertising alcohol and cigarettes to the susceptible young, but persecute and imprison middle-aged women who seek relief from harassment and depression by means of a few amphetamine tablets, as well as adolescent pot-smokers. Such unedifying anomalies reflect little credit on the state or the law, and emphasize the gulf between the generations that is so dangerous and disruptive a phenomenon of contemporary society. The prohibition of cannabis almost certainly does more harm than good. It is ineffective (600 convictions in 1963, 4683 in 1969). It invests a fairly harmless habit with spurious glamour, and those convicted with an aura of martyrdom amongst many of their contemporaries. Legalization of the drug would surely be more realistic than inevitably hopeless attempts to maintain the ban.

The medical profession itself is anything but immune from irrational attitudes to the remarkable benefits of the current revolution in pharmacology. There are today very few clinical situations indeed where the patient should be called on to suffer severe pain of substantial duration. However, an unholy combination of neurotic fear of addiction with the traditional Christian glorification of suffering leads a minority of physicians to practise unjustifiable parsimony in the dispensation of pain-relieving drugs (just to be on the safe side, most doctor-patients take their favourite analgesics into hospital in their sponge-bags, together with their favourite sleeping tablets). Although many heroin addicts blame their habit on the injudicious medical presciption of the drug for some transient painful condition, such attribution is almost invariably bogus: the patterns of drug-use for pleasure and for the relief of pain are as different as chalk from cheese. Heroin, for example, is an unequalled and irreplaceable remedy for the intense paroxysmal pain that sometimes follows an attack of shingles in the elderly patient, but in many years of its regular prescription I have yet to encounter the patient who failed to return the remaining tablets after the pain had—as it practically always does—finally subsided. But professional fears go far beyond the official dangerous drugs, and although the British consumption of medicines is well below the average for the developed world, tirades about the excessive use of sleeping pills, tranquillizers, and antidepressants are an everyday occurrence—coming in the main, it should be noticed, from physicians not immediately concerned with the personal daily management of distressed patients The plain facts are that suitably selected antidepressants offer specific relief of symptoms in the many patients who suffer from genuine (biochemically determined) depressive illness and have no effect on the normal subject, that most tranquillizers are fairly ineffective, but that in some patients whose whole lives have been dominated by constitutional chronic tension and anxiety the difference between invalidism and social effectiveness may be determined entirely by a few daily tablets of amylobarbitone—or one of its more sophisticated substitutes, none of which is demonstrably and consistently superior. With regard to sleeping-pills, *chacun son goût*. The electroencephalogram (EEG) of those who have taken a barbiturate before retiring, we are told, remains abnormal at least until tea-time the next day. The EEG of the sleeping-car traveller denied pharmacological tranquillization may also show changes attributable to sleep deprivation, carefully devised by those railway workers employed to trundle milk-churns down the platform at every halt. The experienced traveller can safely be left to decide whether his alertness the next day is jeopardized more by barbiturate or by sleeplessness, and his judgment in the matter is more reliable than any evidence that can be furnished by the EEG. Incidentally we owe the thalidomide disaster to one of many attempts to find a substitute for the barbiturates, because of their sinister reputation as agents of suicide by overdose—and of course to inexcusable commercial efforts to suppress early reports of the new drug's toxicity. Meanwhile the wide provision of assisted respiration in intensive care units has now reduced the mortality of barbiturate poisoning to vanishing point, unless the victim has taken careful steps to ensure that he will not be found and taken to hospital—or has followed the characteristically thorough Teutonic example of swallowing not twenty or thirty but several hundred tablets. In any case the illogicality of the situation is epitomized by the fact that the candidate for suicide is much likelier to achieve his aim by using aspirin, which is more dangerous in massive dosage and which he can obtain in unlimited quantity without any form of prescription whatever. Most doctors make use of drugs sensibly for non-medical purposes (barbiturates or something similar for sleeplessness, an amphetamine preparation to counteract fatigue under exceptional circumstances) and it seems fairly certain that such use will gradually extend to the general public.

The new pharmacology

Modern pharmacology is a twentieth-century phenomenon and its history presents points of interest to the philosopher of science as well as to the laboratory worker, the physician, and the politician. A few effective drugs are the direct outcome of physiological research. The successful treatment of thyroid deficiency with an extract of the gland in Manchester in 1891 was a very early innovation of this kind; that of diabetes with insulin in 1922 in Toronto probably still the most important. The most recent is the introduction of L-dopa for the treatment of Parkinson's disease: we owe this important therapeutic advance in the main to studies of brain-stem biochemistry provoked by initially empirical observations on the clinical effectiveness of the anti depressive drugs. A handful of significant therapeutic developments have their origin on the other hand in sheer clinical serendipity: until Minot and Murphy in 1926 had the idea of trying raw beef liver (which had recently been demonstrated as the most effective agent of blood regeneration in the dog rendered anaemic by repeated bleeding) on a few patients with pernicious anaemia, the disease was invariably and fairly rapidly fatal. And characteristically enough, the physiologists and biochemists are still arguing about how they did it.

There are other examples in both these categories, but they are the exception. Today most of the important advances in treatment result from the painstaking routine testing of long series of related chemical compounds in the laboratories of the drug industry, especially in Switzerland and the United States. What then is the role of the medical profession? First, it defines the goals and needs of applied pharmacology. There has for example been an avalanche of remedies for stiffness or spasticity determined by lesions of the central nervous system. The patient whose spinal cord has been partially divided, whether in a hunting accident or by a plaque of disseminated sclerosis, needs a drug that will inhibit stiffness and painful nocturnal spasms of the legs without impairing control of the bladder or bowels. The constant procession of new drugs advertised as purveying these virtues is eloquent testimony to their general ineffectiveness. But there are many other clinical demands that the drug industry cannot yet meet: a pain-relieving tablet for arthritis free of the risk of provoking gastro-intestinal haemorrhage that unfortunately characterizes cortisone and phenylbutazone (Butazolidine) as well as the humble aspirin; or a balanced combination of hypnotic and emetic that would preclude successful suicidal overdosage.

Secondly the profession is responsible for the organization of therapeutic trials of drugs developed by the pharmaceutical industry which have passed the stringent tests of animal toxicity now routinely employed, and which there is indirect reason to believe may be therapeutically useful in man. The usual procedure is a pilot test on a handful of intransigent cases followed by a more comprehensive long-term trial, 'double-blind' if possible, carried out in a number of centres. The difficulties of such trials are considerable, and contradictory and equivocal results not uncommon, but there is no alternative. At present their arrangement depends unduly on personal contact and persuasion. There is a good deal to be said for the development of a national panel of reputable investigators, adequately financed by but totally independent of the industry, who would accept this responsibility as their particular contribution to clinical research.

Neither the university departments of pharmacology nor the Medical Research Council have a particularly glorious record in the matter of therapeutic innovation. The former are minuscule. They lack the resources—especially the extensive animal facilities—of the drug houses, and tend either to be absorbed in studies so basic as to be far from application or thrashing round for something useful to do. Belonging to the medical school rather than the hospital, they do not very often give the impression of turning their major attention to the problems of day-to-day practice and therapeutics that preoccupy their clinical colleagues. Much the same applies to the Medical Research Council, the history of which shows a profound bias towards basic as contrasted with clinical science. There has recently been a welcome move from the laboratory to the epidemiological field study, but it is still difficult to escape the impression that the collection of Nobel prizes and the headlong pursuit of the almost metaphysical harvest of molecular biology has taken precedence over the exploitation of science in the service of medicine and man. More obvious evidence of an active interest in therapeutics might possibly have modified Lord Rothschild's depredations?

The pharmaceutical industry attracts a great deal of criticism. especially on the grounds of unduly high prices, excessive profitability, and the duplication of similar or even identical products. Its nationalization has often been mooted. As a convinced socialist I can only say that I would regard such a development as disastrous. Most of the major drug companies are backed by one or other of the mammoths of the general chemical industry, and without commercial resources on this scale it is difficult to conceive of high-risk capital-intensive activities of this order being undertaken at all. In fact pharmaceutical innovation is at some risk at the present time because of the cost and duration of the procedures rightly involved in ensuring, as far as possible, that the drugs marketed are safe for human consumption. Enormous costs in research and development must be met from profits earned chiefly during the few years following the first introduction of a new remedy—and sometimes in competition with a rival firm that enjoys a lead of a few months in familiarizing the professsion with an identical product under its own brand name. Nor does prescription under a chemical rather than a proprietary name ensure either economy or effectiveness: the chemical may be the same, but the physical make-up of the tablet may cause striking variations in the rate of absorption of the drug, its resulting levels in the blood or other tissues, and hence its therapeutic efficacy. The advantage to the physician of using the product of a single reputable company lies in its reliability and the predictability of therapeutic response. The proof of the pudding is in the eating: several eastern European countries have respectable and even massive national pharmaceutical organizations, but it is difficult to think of a single major therapeutic innovation in 25 years that has originated in one of them. Perhaps the drug industry will be the final bastion of competitive capitalism.

Future developments

Prediction in science as in other fields is hazardous because it can be made only in the light of existing knowledge. Prophecies about world oil supplies, for example, have been overturned by the finding of new fields that could not be taken into account within the horizon of the companies' twenty-year trading programmes. In general the projections of such writers as Jules Verne and H. G. Wells have proved closer to the mark than those of their less imaginative scientific contemporaries. Admittedly J. D. Bernal was confident about space exploration as early as 1953, but the conspicuous practical success of some major technological developments like jet propulsion and radar seems to have been almost unexpected. And in a period when the man who split the atom could envisage no conceivable practical application of his achievement, and when no less a person than the Astronomer Royal described space travel as 'bunk' two years before the Sputnik took to the skies, it behoves the worker amongst the many variables of applied biology (for that is what medicine is) to proceed with caution. Even the computer cannot be relied on: it is said that a projection based on trends in horse-drawn traffic in the 1870s would have predicted that by 1970 the surface of the globe would be covered by six feet of manure.

The difficulties of prediction in medical science are inversely proportional to the period of time covered. There is some chance of success over a five-year period, little over a decade, and virtually none over twenty years. This is one of the inescapable problems of medical planning, and means that a continuing series of 'mistakes' is inevitable.

With these reservations I would guess that major short-term developments are most likely to come in the fields of psychopharmacology, virology, the improved control of genetic abnormalities, better techniques of family planning, and possibly though not certainly, cancer.

Psychopharmacology is at present the most important growing point of therapeutics. There are steady improvements in antidepressive therapy, the newer preparations having fewer unpleasant side-effects and acting more rapidly. Until recently there was often a period of up to six weeks before the physician could be certain as to whether a drug such as impramine (Tofranil) would safely control a depressive illness, but today a daily intravenous infusion of clomipramine (Anafranil) will very often assuage even severe depression in ten days and without the troublesome side-effects of electroconvulsive therapy. In schizophrenia a major therapeutic advance has been the introduction of the fluophenazine preparations; a monthly intramuscular injection of Modecate often serves as effective maintenance therapy in relapsing schizophrenics, who because of lack of insight or fecklessness often fail to maintain daily medication on an out-patient basis. There is a long way to go before the drug treatment of schizophrenia achieves the approximately 75 per cent success rate of antidepressant therapy, but progress is continuous and it is not too much to hope that within the next few decades the wards of chronic schizophrenics that still characterize our vast mental hospitals will take their place in medical history with the obsolescent tuberculosis sanatoria. This is one of the most hopeful fields of medical advance, and one we owe to the chemical industry rather than to medicine or psychiatry.

Virology is another growth point of modern medicine. The increasing scope and effectiveness of vaccination against acute viral infections has already been mentioned, though their chemotherapy has so far been much less effective. It has long been known that viruses could also persist in the tissues for many years, giving rise to acute local disease in the presence of a second factor: the virus of *herpes simplex* causes recurrent acute lesions on the lips secondary to upper respiratory tract infections ('cold spots') or sometimes even at the time of menstruation or emotional disturbance. We owe the realization that viruses may cause chronic as well as recurrent acute diseases to studies of a number of diseases of the nervous system including Kuru (a progressive disease encountered in the New Guinea highlands, probably related to the curious custom of eating the brains of departed relatives) and a subacute form of encephalitis due to the measles virus. We are almost certainly at the beginning of a new chapter in medicine dealing with the chronic virus diseases, and although there is little concrete progress to report thus far it obviously raises further possibilities in the use of chemotherapeutic and immunological agents in treatment.

In the field of human reproduction there are several interesting lines of development likely to yield important benefits during the next decade. Genetic engineering in the sense of minute chromosomal adjustments seems far away. However, in suspicious cases examination of the amniotic fluid surrounding the foetus, whether for enzymatic or cytological abnormalities, is likely to reduce the burden of congenital anomalies in some degree by justifying selective abortion. Needless to say, contraception is always preferable to abortion in the general field of family planning, and in this connection it seems likely that the 'morning-after' pill will shortly reduce the requirement for surgical termination of pregnancy.

The enormous resources that have been and are being devoted, so far with scant result, to 'mission-orientated' research into the cause and control of cancer, and our continuing reliance on destructive methods of treatment such as surgery and radiotherapy underline the intrinsic difficulties of the field. In some cases we can identify an exciting cause for the unbridled invasive proliferation of cells that characterises malignant new growth. Tar, X-rays, excessive exposure to ultraviolet light, and the continued inhalation of asbestos particles or cigarette smoke are a few of the more well-known causes of the chronic tissue irritation that leads to cancer in an appreciable proportion of those so exposed, while some avian cancers at any rate are unequivocally caused by virus infection. Since the number of possible chemical agents of cancer production is legion, since their recognition is delayed by the period of years that is required for the development of the pathological changes, and above all since in most human cancers no such agent is identifiable, community protection against cancer except in occasional well-defined instances yields few dividends. Even when substantial dividends could be envisaged, as in the case of tobacco, the difficulties of prevention are self-evident. Emphasis has recently shifted from the virtually uncontrollable multiplicity of potentially carcinogenic agents to the 'host' factor, and in this connection immunological concepts are invoked. The problem is to identify a single biochemical factor concerned in cellular proliferation, whatever its activating cause, in the hope that it can be controlled by chemotherapy or neutralized by immunization. One of the most stimulating concepts of the new immunology is that cancer may be the price the highly developed vertebrate pays for his varied repertoire of cellular differentiation, and that the development of rogue cancer cells is a frequent occurrence, especially during middle and later life, the large majority of them being destroyed by the body's in-built immune protective mechanisms. The fact that the prostate gland, the cervix uteri, the submucous layer of the heavy smoker's bronchial tubes often silently harbour microscopically 'malignant' cells for years before they explode into clinical cancer can be quoted in support of this view. So far however the advances have been conceptual rather than practical, and allowance must be made for a not unnatural tendency to interpret a wide variety of pathological processes in terms of the currently fashionable science of immunology. Immunization against cancer is certainly an attractive idea. Whether such immunization might be general or specific for a particular type of growth is only one of many unsolved questions of a highly problematical situation.

Medical logistics and priorities

Even if we were improbably to heed the muttered injunctions of some timid administrators and try to impose a moratorium on new research and the development of new techniques, or those of some distinguished scientific pessimists and decline to investigate what they arbitrarily regard as better unknown, it is clear that even the application of existing medical knowledge has enormous potentialities for increasing human health and happiness. Of course a moratorium wouldn't work, even if it operated through a selective Rothschild-type diversion of resources to establishment-authenticated activities. Since the Spanish Inquisition failed to quench scientific curiosity it seems unlikely that the British Civil Service would be more successful. As for the philosophical pessimist, he faces the awkward dilemma that the investigator can never envisage the ultimate social implications of his discoveries, whether for good or ill.

The fact remains that the headlong advance of medical science has faced administrators and governments with some extremely difficult problems. And more often than not irrevocable decisions of policy must be taken long before sufficient data are available to permit anything approaching scientific judgement: the institution of population screening for cervical cancer is a recent example. Similarly, thermography of normal women will reveal a certain number of 'hot spots' in one or other breast; is this to be a signal for wholesale surgery for suspected cancer, or for the cold-blooded prospective study that is essential if the real significance of such findings is to be evaluated? Ideally the second alternative is preferable, since it may spare some women unnnecessary operation, while the first may fossilize a non-contributory technique of surgical management and hamper real progress over a period of decades. The susceptibility of such issues to group pressures is self-evident: it also raises ethical problems more appropriate for later discussion.

Total resources

From the start, the cost of the British National Health Service has been far greater than its initiators predicted, and it continues to rise progressively. Some of the reasons for this are simple; for example the service was inaugurated without any serious attempt to estimate the extent of public need for dentures or spectacles, and in the event this proved to be very much greater than had been anticipated. Expectations that easier access to medical attention would diminish sickness and absence from work, and would lead to a decline in demands on the service, were soon shown to be mistaken. It must also be remembered that one reason for its establishment was that the old voluntary hospital system had ceased to be viable: the service inherited a run-down plant. Despite the acceptance of governmental responsibility, our rate of new hospital building since the take-over has unbelievably been slower than under the old system before the war, and the service continues to operate under considerable physical handicaps imposed by old buildings often in the wrong places and quite unsuited to the practice of modern medicine. Finally of course, nobody could foresee the dramatic developments in medical science and technology that were to make such rapidly increasing demands on resources of material and especially of skilled personnel.

The total resource to be devoted to the health service is a matter for political decision by the government of the day and is usually expressed in terms of the gross national product (GNP), of which the NHS at present absorbs something like $5\frac{1}{2}$ per cent. Perhaps because we are not one of the biggest spenders amongst the developed countries in this connection successive Health Ministers fight shy of international comparison, pointing out with some justification that such figures cannot be regarded as strictly comparable when there are such wide differences between the various countries concerned in their methods of delivering and financing medical care, as well as in the extent of the private sector and the amount of self-medication undertaken outside the organized service. What is certain is that the percentage of GNP devoted to medicine is steadily increasing in every developed country and that it will inevitably continue to increase in the measurable future. It will be politically impracticable entirely to deny an increasingly affluent public, with increasing expectations, the benefits of the new developments in medical science that they see so vividly portrayed on their television screens. However, there has already been one post-war period (1950–5) during which the percentage of the gross national product devoted to the NHS in Britain actually decreased, and it is disquieting to note that despite the scientific revolution in medicine, and the increasing needs starkly evident from existing demographic data, the last Labour Chancellor, Mr. Jenkins, cheerfully predicted a substantial decline in the rate of increase in health services expenditure in his financial forecasts of 1969. However, expenditure on health is more acceptable to the electorate than spending on some other governmental activities, and uninhibited projection of present expenditure trends would point to the non-sensical conclusion that within a hundred years medicine will absorb 100 per cent of our GNP. Presumably the critical level will be somewhere between the present $5\frac{1}{2}$ and 100 per cent, but it is likely to be at least 10 per cent well before the end of the present century. Indeed this figure has already been approached in more than one developed country where medicine enjoys a higher priority than in Britain.

The medical services are in competition with education, housing, and defence in the matter of resources, and the physician has the right of any citizen to press the claims of his particular interest, but experience suggests that he exerts little influence on the outcome. The medical profession has however one further social duty—to indicate the magnitude of need and the nature of deficiencies if the declared national goal of a comprehensive and effective health service is to be achieved and maintained. The size of the problem can best be illustrated by considering one small but well-defined sector where a serious attempt has been made to estimate need, curiously enough in France, a country not renowned for its medical administration. These figures emerged in the course of a study on rehabilitation, a field of medical activity neglected in Britain but a focus of active interest in the EEC, partly perhaps because several of its members happily face a shortage rather than a superfluity of labour. They concern head injury, an area in which both incidence and severity can be assessed with reasonable accuracy. Because of increasing industrialization and road traffic this presents growing problems in every developed and developing country: indeed trauma like lung cancer and self-poisoning, is a contemporary epidemic. The French estimate is that 250 000 head injuries receive medical attention in France each year, of which 50 000 require hospital admission. Many of the larger number must be relatively trivial. Efficient rehabilitation of all head injuries of moderate or more than moderate severity ould need 160 rehabilitation beds per million of population as compared with 500 per million required for the rehabilitation of general illnesses and injuries. These figures are of course astronomical in relation to any rehabilitation facilities at present envisaged in Britain. However, allowing for different criteria for hospital admission determined by the extent of facilities and the pattern of practice, extrapolation to Britain would not be entirely fallacious. In 1968, for example, nearly 120 000 patients were discharged from or died in hospitals in England and Wales as a result of head injury, and every day there were about 2000 in-patients in hospital because of its immediate effects. The social wastage of head injury arises less from the relatively small number of patients with severe brain damage (some of whom, incidentally, do remarkably well in the long term), but in the prolonged and demoralizing loss of work that all too often follows fairly minor industrial injury in patients discharged from hospital after a few days to a sometimes uninformed, inexpert, and over-anxious general practitioner, in a setting of impending litigation. These are the patients who need immediate and vigorous rehabilitation, and experience in a truly comprehensive medical service such as that of the war-time Royal Air Force demonstrated that under appropriate conditions, and with motivational encouragement, most could return to work within a few weeks instead of the one or two years that is so regrettably common in medico-legal cases. However, to furnish facilities for the rehabilitation of head injuries in Britain on the scale envisaged—though not yet undertaken—in France would demand no less than 8000 places in head injury rehabilitation centres. In fact facilities of this kind in Britain hardly exist at all. Again, Virchow's aphorism about medicine and politics is apposite. When labour is short it is cherished. With a social system that tolerates three-quarters of a million unemployed, the salvaging of the head-injured may on the surface seem an extravagance. In fact of course it is not extravagant, because the cost of sick benefit, litigation, and compensation outweighs the short-term expense of rehabilitation.

Allocations and priorities

The medical profession has more to contribute to issues of allocation and priorities than to deliberations on total allotment. Even priorities however are not immune from political pressures, and, incidentally, one interesting new development in this situation is the emergence during the past decade of an increasing number of pressure groups of sufferers from particular chronic diseases—and especially their families—who publicize the needs of their particular group and also stimulate and subsidize research, but who are at some risk of using their resources to distort the application of total research potential.

Information on cost-effectiveness and cost benefit of medical care is scanty and unreliable. Some sort of estimate of the cost of a course of treatment can certainly be made, though exactly what is included and what is omitted in its assessment (for example the capital cost of building) renders it little more than arbitrary, and an insecure basis for comparative studies. The assessment of effectiveness and benefit is infinitely more difficult. Such studies as have been attempted have usually relied on easily measured objective parameters such as length of stay in hospital and duration of absence from work. Pain and suffering, or the ultimate qualitative results of medical or surgical treatment, lend themselves less easily to quantification. Nevertheless the attempt should be made, and it ought to be made by a number of teams each comprising an experienced and spontaneously interested physician and others with skills in social work, economics and accountancy. The Department of Health would have much to gain from the establishment of a few pilot departments of medical economics on these lines in selected medical schools, and the component of clinical professionalism would help to avert the main risk of such studies, which is missing the wood for the trees by relying entirely on what is easily measurable at the expense of what may be more important but less tangible.

In the matter of allocation one thing is clear: under any conceivable system, demand, fortified by continuing advance, will always outstrip available resources. Always there will be new methods of treatment which cannot and should not be available, except on a limited experimental scale and in a few centres, until their value has been clearly demonstrated. However when this stage has been passed and a method of treatment (such as dialysis and transplantation for chronic kidney disease) has been firmly established as life-saving, the profession and the public can be excused some degree of impatience if the provision of general access to the new facility for all those who could be saved by it is not given high priority. However, the implications of such policy decisions are underlined by the recent observation of a French economist that if the waiting-list for dialysis in his country was cleared overnight, the total cost would equal that of the rest of France's health service.

Personnel

To the writer the most remarkable single indictment of the National Health Service is that 23 years after its institution his own Hospital Region relies on medical graduates from India and Pakistan for no less than 75 per cent of its junior hospital staff, that national figures not far short of this have been accepted with equanimity by a long succession of Health Ministers, and that even today the steps being taken to remedy the situation are too little, too late, and unlikely to have any impact for ten years at the very earliest. The United States relies similarly on graduates from South Korea and Puerto Rico, but the United States at any rate frankly accepts the anarchy implicit in a free market for medical care, and makes no pretence of operating a 'comprehensive medical health service, free and open to all'. Our hospital service operates by courtesy of the medical schools of Madras and Bombay, and if this source of imported labour were to peter out it would collapse. At the turn of the century many an ambitious young British surgeon sought an appointment in India because it afforded easy and extensive operative experience on an under-doctored native population. Today the tables are turned. The graduate of Lahore or Dacca comes here to learn his skills on British patients, as well as to acquire one of the higher professional diplomas the manufacture of which constitutes a minor national industry and—unless he marries here and settles in one of the consultant vacancies freely available in many branches of an understaffed hospital service, or leaves for the more lucrative pastures of North America—to return to one of the metropolitan centres of the Indian subcontinent and exploit his experience and highly valued qualifications in the field of private practice that furnishes the only feasible setting for the practice of modern medicine in such a society. The postgraduate training of Asian graduates is of course an unexceptionable contribution to medicine that Britain is well-equipped to undertake, though what is taught and learned is not always entirely relevant to the Asian situation. But quite apart from the fact that the supply will dry up as Indian postgraduate facilities develop, and that these people are badly needed to man the fragmentary health services of their own countries, it is shameful that we should have to rely on them to under-pin medical care in our infinitely more affluent society.

The prediction of manpower needs is notoriously difficult, and even in what seems at first sight a circumscribed field like medicine its record of success is anything but impressive. However there can be no doubt that we do not train enough doctors to man our service at its present level, and equally certain that need will increase with an ageing population and the development of new and always labour-intensive medical techniques. The steps that have been taken to meet this situation have been and remain ludicrously inadequate —two new medical schools in the better part of a century. Hypnotized by the eighteenth-century chimera of non-vocational education, the new universities have taken little interest in the professional schools that formed the base of European university development. In Britain this also reflects in part the fact that the Health Department has no responsibility for recruiting or training those who will staff its services. This responsibility lies firmly on the doorstep of the Department of Education and Science by way of the University Grants Committee. This body gives a distinct impression of regarding medical education as an unruly and unrewarding burden only marginally less expensive (and much less respectable) than big-scale physics, and in unfair competition with archaeology and Sanskrit. The situation in eastern Europe is otherwise. There the Health Minister is responsible for staffing his service and for both undergraduate and postgraduate medical education. The prosecution of medical education in state academies rather than universities has its disadvantages, and one or two communist countries run a mixed system, but even if it means that medical students must be trained without the cultural benefits claimed to result from humanizing contact with departments of medieval history and philosophy it has at any rate the virtue that somebody—in this case the Health Minister—is responsible for matching need and supply in the matter of provision of professional services.

Nursing
Steadily mounting problems of nursing recruitment and staffing

occasion increasing concern, and have recently begun to affect not only the peripheral hospitals but also the large centrally situated teaching hospitals which have traditionally had a wide choice of good candidates. Despite a series of salary increases over a period of years, nurses are still not well remunerated considering the skills required and the responsibilities undertaken. Nevertheless the problems seem to be sociological rather than purely financial. Before the Second World War nursing was one of the relatively few appropriate occupations freely open to the intelligent young woman: it also had the advantages of offering experience of city life under sheltered circumstances to girls brought up in the country and of equipping them to fill a valued role in society when they returned after marriage, for example to a farming community. Today, however, there is a wide variety of occupations open to young women. In many they can earn more than nurses after briefer training, with less responsibility, less discipline, and above all much less irregular and inconvenient hours of work.

Already there are signs that we are sliding towards a situation deplorably familiar in the United States, where a few professional nurses (some of them 'graduate' nurses with relatively little day-to-day nursing experience) act as ward manageresses controlling teams of relatively untrained staff of variable quality. The professional nurse has very little direct patient contact indeed. The results are unattractive, especially for the patient. The traditional British pattern has been that of the professional ward, theatre or casualty sister, working almost autonomously with the medical staff of the unit to which she has a long-term attachment, and with a minimum of central administrative interference. This system is still marginally viable in the best institutions, but elsewhere it is gravely threatened by general staff shortages; a decreasing supply of first-class sisters because of earlier marriage; extensive reliance on part-time nurses at every level; and the further breaching of continuity of care by the application of the 40-hour week, which is about as appropriate for the nurse as it would be for the housewife.

The problem is intractable. The main step taken towards its amelioration by the Health Department is the application of the recommendations of the Salmon Report, which virtually remodel the staffing structure of the nursing profession and which it is hoped will render it more attractive. The Department continues to preach the virtues of the scheme, which most of the medical profession regards as an unmitigated disaster; meanwhile recruiting continues to present serious difficulties except in a few rural or industrially depressed areas where alternative employment is hard to come by—and paradoxically it is in these areas that exiguous hospital budgets sometimes lead to unemployment amongst those trained. The Salmon Report was drawn up by a committee under the chairmanship of a distinguished businessman from the world of mass catering, heavily loaded with senior representatives of nursing organisations, and without a single working nurse as a member. Its recommendations were geared to appeal to the nursing administration to whom it offers considerable increases in status and salary. It replaces the traditional titles of sister and matron by nursing officer grade 6 and nursing officer grade 9 and more important than this, it erodes the professional autonomy of the ward sister (grade 6 in the new terminology) by appointing a 'grade 7' to breathe down the necks of a group of 'grade sixes'. Worse still, since professional and financial advancement depends on upgrading, the very best nurses in theatres and wards have a positive incentive to give up nursing and divert into administration—a procedure as sensible as taking the hospital's best surgeon and appointing him hospital secretary. It seems unlikely that Salmon will have any beneficial effect on recruitment except perhaps of potential administrators. In the meantime the British tradition of entrusting professional matters to intelligent amateurs has been happily maintained by the prosecution of a further inquiry into nursing under the chairmanship of a historian. Mainly concerned with the problems of nurse training and recruitment, the recommendations of the Briggs committee are rather more realistically geared to the professional traditions of nursing than those of its predecessor.

What *should* be done, within whatever organizational framework is finally decided? The most important single step would be to consolidate the nurse's status as a professional member of the medical team, to give her full professional responsibility within it, exercised in collaboration with her medical colleagues, and to ensure that a first-class ward, theatre, or casualty sister does not have to abandon nursing to spend her time filling in forms in order to qualify for the higher levels of salary within the profession. Nursing in the traditional British sense offers a deeply satisfying career, but the combination of immediate personal responsibility for patients and highly skilled technical competence that is required today demands adequate financial reward. The sister who runs an intensive care or dialysis unit is undertaking a responsibility far more arduous and harrowing than that of her administrative superior and should be rewarded accordingly. Salmon's perpetuation of the system of full-time nursing teachers—also supported by the Briggs Report—might have been specifically designed to ensure that what is taught is already out of date, which it does to perfection. Only those actively engaged in practical nursing, with its continually developing technological demands, are fit to teach it. With regard to recruitment, nursing should learn from the army and emphasize how personal, responsible, and difficult the job is, and how well worth doing—together with appropriate stress on much improved remuneration.

To revert to the general difficulties of staffing the NHS, these are certainly soluble, but not in isolation from the general problems of our society. What sort of confidence does a political system engender that misuses the tremendous potential benefits of increasing productivity not to strengthen the under-manned service industries—amongst which the care of people is the most deeply rewarding—but to impose enforced idleness on nearly a million people while many of the rest work overtime?

General practice

Although the British Medical Association and the Department of Health are at one in contending that general practice is the backbone of the NHS, although the resources allocated to this part of the service have been increased, although both the quantity and the quality of recruitment to general practice has been stimulated by increased remuneration, and despite the emergence of an active Royal College and changes of nomenclature (family medicine, primary medical care) there is still uneasiness about the future of general practice in the United Kingdom.

For those who enjoy the pleasures of living in remote areas, whether in the Scottish highlands or along the fjords of Norway, there is and can be no alternative to the local general practitioner, and access to the more sophisticated techniques of modern medicine depends as much on good communications as on the high standard of clinical skill that so often characterizes the doctor who chooses to work in such an environment. The problem really concerns the much larger number of people who live in the cities and large towns, and it is common to all the developed countries. Modern pharmacology has put powerful therapeutic weapons into the hands of even the most isolated physicians, but the medical triumphs and the dramatic developments of the past quarter-century have been centred on the hospitals, and in the public mind these represent the focal centre of modern medicine. This is reflected in the lion's share of finance they have enjoyed since the institution of the Health Service, and in the continuing attraction of a hospital career for the best students. Despite current enthusiasms for Health Centres and 'health teams', the company of biochemists and geneticists remains more stimulating and more attractive to the young medical man than that of social workers and chiropodists.

The theory of British general practice is that the GP is a personal physician of first instance, constantly available, and intimately acquainted with the socio-economic and emotional background of his patients and their families. He also provides the channel of reference to the specialist (the referral arrangement is an integral component of the system), and a valuable protection against the specialist's possibly excessive enthusiasms. In a lifetime of busy consultant practice I have met about a score of GPs who measured up to this exacting specification and several hundred whose level of work was very different. Indeed it is doubtful if this standard of general practice ever applied except to the upper middle class (the very rich and influential often use a consultant general physician as a personal doctor) and in a few curious enclaves like some dale and colliery villages where the patriarchal role of the local doctor represented a valued and highly authoritarian tradition. Everywhere today the situation is changed. There are some parts of Britain where a small town cannot attract a practitioner of any kind. There are many districts, especially in big cities, where group practices, consultations by appointment, commuting practitioners and emergency call services have shattered the element of continuity that is the essence of traditional general practice and have fragmented the provision of primary medical care. In the metropolis especially, the patient's clinical records are often inaccessible in the evening to the Australian or Nigerian postgraduate who is deputizing for the absent GP, and who must make immediate and important clinical decisions without essential background information. Most general practitioners enjoy the benefits of duty rosters, and much more free time than their consultant colleagues in under-staffed regional hospitals, who are not infrequently on almost permanent call except for their annual holiday.

Of course the rationalization implicit in group practice, health centres and organized off-duty has kept the system in operation, and there is more optimism on the subject today than there was a few years ago—largely due, it must be admitted, to manipulation of the only real variable, which is improved remuneration. But doubts remain. Except for the Netherlands and to some extent Austria, Britain is the only developed country where general provision of the personal general practitioner service still obtains: elsewhere the growth of specialized knowledge and the difficulties in the way of the effective generalist are recognized. In the great cities of the United States virtually all clinical practice is specialized, and home visiting virtually non-existent. Sweden probably has the world's most efficient medical service, and it is run with proportionately fewer doctors than our own. They practise in modern purpose-built properly equipped premises and are extremely well paid for long hours of solid work with patients, brought to them by ambulance if necessary, rather than for motoring from one domiciliary visit to another; follow-up visiting is done by nurses. In eastern Europe most primary medical care is dispensed from district specialist polyclinics. It is interesting that in Yugoslavia such polyclinics initially employed general practitioners to guide the patients into the appropriate specialist channel, but this system has gradually declined as patients proved quite capable of choosing their own specialist. The North American, Swedish, and east European systems of furnishing the doctor of first instance differ, and none would be entirely appropriate to British conditions. However, the possible need for change in our traditional system of general practice combined with specialist referral, firmly based on more than two centuries of professional differentiation between shopkeeper-apothecary and university-trained physician, must be faced. In several parts of the world, group general practice has been modified by clinical specialization within the group, and this system has many adherents amongst the livelier and younger general practitioners in Britain. Its disadvantages are that it tends to create two classes of specialist —the genuine specialist and the 'specialoid'; that the information explosion is such that even the most highly specialized doctor has continual difficulty in keeping abreast of his field; and that the semi-specialist is easily tempted to undertake duties beyond his capacity.

On the other hand it cannot be denied that many patients at present referred to specialists in hospital are suffering from trivial disorders that could be easily and effectively treated at a less sophisticated level. These issues are controversial and unresolved. In general it seems unlikely that conditions in Britain are so different from those obtaining in other industrialized countries that general practice will survive in its traditional form, or that enough doctors can be made available to furnish an effective two-tier system of medical care for the whole population. The semi-specialist is looked on with well-founded suspicion by most of the profession, and there are some who would regard a reversal of this position as more realistic in the long term—that most clinicians should be specialists, but that they should all have had sufficient training in general medicine in the broad sense to share in the provision of primary medical care. This could benefit specialist skills without diluting specialist competence. Traditional professional objections to this kind of doctor practising from a specialist polyclinic are numerous and powerful. Many general practitioners contend that the patient is not fit to choose his specialist, that the unsatisfactory nature of such an arrangement is clearly evident in the United States, and that the specialist in turn is less competent than the generalist to direct the patient with an illness outside his field to a more appropriate channel of care and investigation. However, the imperfections of medical care in the United States are more closely related to the financial conditions of practice than to self-selection of the specialist. One danger of our system is the generalist who wrongly thinks himself competent to deal with a serious and complicated case, or who may be entirely unaware of what modern medicine has to offer in an unusual illness, and fails to refer the patient along the line. The good general practitioner will of course discern his patient's wish for a second opinion and take the initiative, but it is not very uncommon for a specialist consultation to be sought in the teeth of the practitioner's objections and his more often than not erroneous assurance that the consultant's specialized knowledge can contribute nothing to the patient's situation. The specialist is more likely to appreciate his limitations and less reluctant to seek specialized help for a patient outside his field than the optimistic generalist. And although it is not long since Lord Moran stirred up a hornet's nest by daring to suggest that consultants were usually recruited from amongst the most academically able and intelligent students, this is still the case despite the attractions of the 'health team'. The fear carefully nurtured by generations of practitioners that the specialist's clinical perspective is constricted is not usually well founded, and the patient with a complaint of short sight who wanders by accident into the clinic of a rectal surgeon is more likely to end up with a pair of spectacles than an operation for piles.

The respective roles of general practitioner and consultant have recently been the subject of pungent review in a Maurice Bloch Lecture delivered at Glasgow University by Richard Crossman. This illustrates very well some common attitudes of politicians to the problems of health service organization: well-justified fears of the increasing cost of adequate hospital provision; a characteristically paranoid conviction that hospitals operate for the convenience of doctors rather than for service to patients; and a rather rosy view of what can be expected of the general practitioner. The former Secretary of State rightly stresses the relative neglect of chronic hospital facilities; the continuing role of the small simple community hospital; and the inevitable dependence of the service on money raised by taxation by comparison with the trivial contribution that can be expected either from public charges or from private practice in any imaginable future. He attacks the professional emphasis on major as opposed to minor but easily treatable illness, and raises another controversy central to the whole issue of the NHS—the role of the local authorities. In keeping with Labour Party policy he feels that some measure of control by elected representatives keeps the service in closer touch with patient and community needs. This view is not shared by the medical profession, which has found over the years that nominated Boards of Governors of Teaching Hospitals have on the whole been more responsible, less parochial, and better informed than Regional Hospital Boards with their element of district representation. Refreshment of the membership of a nominated board takes into account the board's needs in the way of expertise as well as the personal contribution the member would be able to make. Only a professional politician could really believe that such qualities are especially likely to be found amongst the restricted and self-selected group of people who have submitted to the capricious judgement of the hustings, and the profession is grateful to Mr. Crossman's successor for not having thrown it to the local authorities.

Community Medicine

The concepts of community medicine and the community physician are very much in the news at the moment, though they are concepts that markedly lack clear definition. Their origin can be traced to the decline of the local authority Public Health Services occasioned by the creation of the NHS. Medical Officers of Health who had been sufficiently energetic and able to influence enlightened councils to create hospitals within the unpromising environment of the workhouse lost them overnight to the Regional Hospital Board, which also took over clinical responsibility for infectious diseases, which twenty years ago still accounted for an important volume of illness, especially in the young. The MOH was left with responsibility for the collection and presentation of the rather limited public health statistics routinely collected in his community, for the supervision of some personal preventive services, such as child welfare and the school medical services, and for the organization of ambulance, home help, and home nursing services. Except for a handful of outstanding individuals in each generation Medical Officers of Health have always tended to be both a depressed and a rather depressing section of the profession, and it is not surprising that the opportunities for large-scale administration offered by the creation of the Regional Hospital Boards seduced many of the best men from the local authority service. Since this time the position has further deteriorated in that the implementation of the Seebohm Report has led the MOH to surrender control of the social services previously under his direction to an army of professional social workers. The long-term implications of this change are still not clear. The contention of the social workers and their representatives is that medical officers were unsuited to the organization and supervision of the social services, which had become a highly professional exercise. It may be that some of the present troubles in this sector will be temporary, but they are certainly considerable. There is a quite inadequate number of properly trained social workers to carry out the multifarious duties envisaged for them, while the functional and administrative separation between the social worker and the clinician is accentuated by the fact that each is working for a different employer: the Seebohm Report creates an artificial and quite illogical division between medical and social care. It is difficult to escape the impression that the social services were left in the hands of local authorities rather than of the Regional Hospital

Boards (or their successors) in order to give the local authorities a function in this area rather than because of any real merit in the arrangement. It is to be hoped that the impending replacement of Regional Boards by Area Health Authorities with wider functions will improve the quality and amount of epidemiological and statistical information available to the NHS, but it will put another nail in the coffin of the MOH, who as such will virtually become extinct by 1974. This has been one impetus to the provision of the community physician. The second reason for the current popularity of the concept concerns the organizational inadequacy of the health service in general and of general practice in particular, and the difficulties of communication between the general practice and hospital sides of the service. Twenty years ago the traditional pattern worked well enough. The hospital consultant serviced a group of general practitioners in his particular field, who referred their occasional private patient to him and as a *quid pro quo* were able to call on his personal services for their hospital patients. The domiciliary consultations provided for under the Health Service were a valuable social meeting-point and served an educative as well as a clinical function. Unfortunately they have declined in popularity. They are time-consuming, and although consultants rarely decline to undertake them, many practitioners prefer to send their patient direct to hospital with a hastily scribbled note, to be exasperated days or weeks later by the patient's return home, often in advance of the hospital report that is a necessary basis for subsequent management.

It is envisaged that the community physician will in some not entirely clear way have a brief to consider these and other problems of integration and seek ways of overcoming them. In most of the schemes so far envisaged he will have little or no clinical responsibility, but will be responsible for identifying areas of needs and organizing lines of communication, especially in connection with the management of those chronic illnesses that have a tendency to slip from medical notice once they have lasted for some time. In one sense this function represents an echo of the demand for better management in medicine which has been so frequently enunciated by the present government, and a recognition by some elements in the profession that if it is not provided by doctors, it is likely to be wished on them by statistician–managers.

Despite much discussion about the community physician it must be admitted that his role remains in many ways uncertain, and it is not easy to envisage a flood of good professional recruits to work of this nature. It might furnish appropriate employment for a man who has spent his medical career in the armed forces, but the present tendency in this field is to retain the medical officers who are worth retaining for as long as they are able to render effective service, and their recruitment even for attractive appointments is anything but easy.

Hospitals

The under-capitalization that has hampered the NHS since its inception is evident to anyone who cares to tour the hospitals of his neighbourhood, the average age of which he will probably find to be about seventy years. In most larger towns there will be an ex-voluntary hospital, possibly dating from the early years of the present century, which has been extended and partially renovated piecemeal over the years. The other major institution is likely to be an ex-workhouse of older vintage and more dreary aspect. If he happens to drive round the thriving conurbation of Teesside—the site of Europe's largest chemical industrial complex—he will find no less than 23 hospitals, nearly all hopelessly out of date and uneconomic in operation, which might have been specifically arranged so as to ensure that their consultant staff spends more time travelling between them than working inside them. The cost of rectifying two decades of neglected hospital building will be so astronomical as to ensure that radical physical reconstruction will not be completed within half a century at the earliest, by which time needs will have changed and hospitals at present under construction will be obsolescent candidates for early demolition. The interminable delay between planning and execution has proved as disastrous as shortage of money, though experience in other countries and indeed in wartime Britain clearly reveals that it is neither an act of God nor an inevitable concomitant of reconstructing a hospital system. In the most northerly regional board area of England, which is responsible for the hospital services of a population of 3 250 000, one new general hospital was built during the first 20 years of the service. It was opened to patients 12 years after planning began and it is in the wrong place. The fact that it is also badly and extravagantly designed is probably not unconnected with the scant experience any British architect now in practice has had in hospital design and construction during his working lifetime. There are faint signs of improvement in this deplorable situation during the past few years, but they are too faint for comfort and there is little evidence of any sense of urgency. It is interesting to speculate on the reasons for the striking contrast between the very large number of new schools that have been built since the end of the Second World War and the tiny number of hospitals. The country is covered with a rash of glass-walled primary and secondary schools in which pupils can be roasted alive in summer and frozen to death in winter, but the poor-law institution turned hospital more often than not has to make do with tasteless internal redecoration and inadequate augmentation of its primitive lavatory accommodation. This disparity may of course not be unconnected with the question of cost. The capital cost of a primary school place at present is £296, that of a bed in an old people's home £4000, and that of a bed in a district general hospital more than £10 000.

But the difficulties of the hospital situation are not merely financial. Three others at least deserve special mention: the relation between hospital and community care that is especially important in relation to the management of psychiatric illness; changing views on the optimal size of hospitals; and the particular difficulties of some long-neglected sectors of the hospital service. The idea of a steady replacement of institutional treatment by community care for mental illness has made considerable headway in recent years, facilitated by the extensive introduction of simple treatment of even serious mental illness with drugs which can return most depressives and many schizophrenics to the community with relative safety, even if not always with unimpaired social effectiveness. Amongst the other reasons for this development are the appalling conditions that obtain in the vast overcrowded and under-doctored wards of some of the older mental hospitals and, to central governments, its anticipated contribution to economy. However there is considerable anxiety in psychiatric circles over two aspects of this move. First, its success depends on the organization of adequate community services that are largely the responsibility of local authorities, which often manifest very little interest in furnishing them, together with a reluctance to undertake responsibilities and expenditure they feel should really be an obligation of the nationally financed hospital service. Secondly, although the extent of hospital provision required for depression has been diminished by modern treatment, and while that for schizophrenia is likely to show some reduction, this is likely to be more than counterbalanced by the exponential demand of psychogeriatrics. Finally, the cost of hospital care must be weighed against that of maintaining the partially recovered psychiatric casualty in the family circle. Most patients prefer to be at home, but every doctor knows families that have been socially and economically crippled by the burden of coping with such an invalid. It will certainly be inexcusable if the move from hospital to community care is made before adequate community care is organized, and although parts of our traditional mental hospital system may be closed down in the measurable future, especially with steadily improving psychiatric facilities for short-term cases in general hospitals, others will undoubtedly require adaptation for the care of the elderly chronic psychiatric patient who is an increasing burden at every level of the health service.

Optimum hospital size remains a controversial topic. The present Secretary of State has gone on record as being opposed to the very large hospital complex, and there is no doubt that he speaks for a considerable proportion and probably a majority of the lay public. Indeed, the threatened closure of any local hospital, however small and however disadvantageous for effective operation, in favour of more rational central provision, can be guaranteed to arouse public uproar. However, many in the medical profession take the opposite view, and it is not insignificant that the sick or injured doctor will take infinite trouble to get to the nearest large medical centre, even though it may mean goading the ambulance driver to pass a series of small institutions. It is quite impossible for example, for such hospitals to provide 24-hour resident and radiological coverage. The standard size accepted by the Health Ministry for a district general hospital from 1948 until the last few years was 600 to 1000 beds. This figure was perfectly appropriate for 1939 when the wards were occupied by medical, surgical, gynaecological, and orthopaedic patients with a handful of beds for other specialties. This figure is now recognized to be too low for a hospital that can offer a comprehensive service, and although no official statement on the subject is available the impression is that something like 1200 to 1500 beds may be considered more realistic. Specialization of function is a fact of life, and a moment's consideration will demonstrate the inadequacy even of this scale for a major medical centre. If we take a simple example, a 24-hour neurosurgical service—which is absolutely essential if head injuries and intracranial haemorrhage are to be adequately dealt with—demands the provision of four surgical teams, each with a neurosurgeon and his assistants, a specially experienced anaesthetist, a neuroradiologist, and all the nursing, ancillary, and laboratory workers required to give the patient the benefit of modern methods. Such teams work an eight-hour shift in practice, but a fourth team is essential to cover holidays and occasional absences. Such an arrangement would be quite uneconomic if it serviced less than 120 acute beds. A regional neurosurgical unit smaller than this is bound to fall short of full efficiency, and signalizes the abandonment of any serious attempt to give the public the benefits that new knowledge and new techniques have to offer. The situation is identical in several other specialities, such as thoracic surgery, major trauma, plastic surgery, and orthopaedics. A few years ago it was suggested that each district general hospital should sponsor one or other of these special units on a realistic scale, but the lesson of the current epidemic of road injuries is that the patient who needs expert orthopaedic treatment is also the patient quite likely to need the attention of a neurosurgeon and a thoracic surgeon. The practice of modern medicine and surgery demands that all special skills must be available day and night on the same site, and this requires a unit of at the very least 2000 beds and almost certainly more.

Needless to say there are less densely populated regions where such provision would be impracticable and where a hospital of 200 to 500 beds must meet the needs of the area, with prompt transfer to the nearest major centre in any case requiring special treatment. There is also, as the Secretary of State has recently pointed out, still a distinct place for the small community hospital (the old cottage hospital) which can cope with illnesses requiring nothing more than nursing or terminal care, near at hand and with convenient local staff recruitment on a part-time basis. But for serious and complicated medicine and surgery there is no alternative to the large unit served by an effective communication and transport system. The idea that a loss of personal contact and intimacy is an essential feature of such an organization is fallacious. Large hospitals, like large cities, are broken down functionally and socially into village communities, and the atmosphere and friendliness of a ward or unit is determined by the staff relations rather than by the size of the hospital complex.

Population screening

Critics of the NHS often bewail its neglect of preventive medicine and describe it pejoratively as a 'national ill-health service'. Castigating the unreality of medical education that concerns itself with disease-entities rather than 'positive health', and is based on the application of scientific biology rather than on such concepts as 'stress', 'community medicine', 'man in his social environment', and 'the conflict of interpersonal relationships', it is more than likely that such a critic will claim that modern medicine focuses all its attention on illness, and ignores the enormously greater volume of disease in the community that exists unrecognized below the water-line of this metaphorical iceberg. What is contended is that the physician wrongly concentrates his attention on patients who come to him with symptoms, that is, patients in whom disease is already manifest in some degree of disability. He would, in the critic's view, be more profitably occupied in combing his community for pre-symptomatic disease—for pathological abnormalities that have not yet come to the patient's notice or caused any disablement—so that he can deal with them earlier and more effectively.

However, this simple proposition begs a series of crucial questions. How strong is the evidence that pre-symptomatic diagnosis and treatment will improve the patient's chances? How reliable are our methods of diagnosis in the absence of symptoms? How often will cases be missed, evoking a false sense of security? How often will 'false positives' be found, occasioning the further expense of exhaustive investigations, and sometimes perhaps even injudicious treatment? How practical is it to keep a community under continuous scrutiny either for one disease or a group of diseases? And if it is practicable, does it represent a more economic or a more extravagant use of limited resources than, for example, educating the public to recognize certain important early symptoms as signalling an urgent need for professional attention?

The conflict of medical priorities implicit in these discussions finds expression in a powerful lobby in favour of population screening, especially in the United States. Controversy concerns population screening, and not the generally accepted exploitation of laboratory automation to undertake multiple routine biochemical screening tests on patients admitted to hospital: a population of this kind has of course already been clinically selected. The value of screening of potential recruits for special functions is also beyond question: it is vitally important to know the physiological responses of potential astronauts, and at a more everyday level to ensure that railway-engine drivers or signalmen are not colourblind. The justification for screening business executives is of a somewhat different order. It is certainly not that they comprise an especially infirm or vulnerable sector of the population. Often a free regular overhaul is presented to them as a valuable gift from the employing company. In fact its most valuable function is exactly the same as that served by the routine examination of senior officers in the armed forces, and concerns the subject's fitness for his duties and the possible need to train a replacement. A mild increase of blood pressure, some over-indulgence in alcohol, or evidence of psychiatric abnormality may be minor and may not even require treatment. From the point of view of the organization, however, they may well raise the question of selecting a possible successor.

But what is under discussion here is a different matter—the screening of a total population, not as a tool of epidemiological research, or to discover the prevalence of particular illnesses in the community, but to detect individuals affected by asymptomatic disease with a view to arranging appropriate treatment or management.

This concept of population screening received a very powerful stimulus from the application of mass miniature radiography to seek out clinical cases—and sources of infection—in the national campaign against pulmonary tuberculosis that followed the introduction of effective chemotherapy for this disease 25 years ago. This campaign was conspicuously successful. The method of case-finding was very reliable. It was practicable in terms of resources of equipment and personnel. It also had the overriding advantage that the form of treatment afforded to the tuberculosis patient detected by it was highly effective and had a convincing success rate. Unfortunately these considerations do not apply to many of the screening techniques so widely publicized at present. In some instances, for example, diagnostic categories are too vague and too subjective to permit clear distinction of the abnormal and the treatable from the very wide range of 'normal' variations. This difficulty arises in the case of psychiatric screening. In other contexts the battery of elaborate tests required for early diagnosis are too expensive to permit regular periodic coverage of the population at risk, as in the case of cancer of the breast. At the other end of the scale, lung cancer can probably be detected in many early cases by the same radiographic techniques that were successfully employed in the early diagnosis of pulmonary tuberculosis, but with only a one-in-twenty chance of five-year survival even after first-class treatment the exercise would pay a poor dividend in the form of an improved outlook for the patient.

There are two special practical difficulties that bedevil decision-making in this field. The first is that medical innovators are usually enthusiasts and seldom excel in critical evaluation. Firmly convinced that their new technique is unquestionably beneficial, they cannot bring themselves to deny the public its benefits during the period of several years' stringent testing that would be required to validate it—or even, to put it bluntly, to make quite sure that they are not really doing more harm than good. From this springs the second difficulty: the new but still unproved method is not only introduced into practice by its progenitors but attracts wide publicity. Demand is created, and pressures from specially interested sections of the profession and from the public lead to premature policy decisions. Once the still unauthenticated technique is incorporated into routine practice, even by a minority of the profession, it is virtually impossible to conduct the controlled trial that alone can furnish truly reliable evaluation, since the deliberate exclusion of some people from its hypothetical benefits can so easily be pilloried as unethical.

Screening for cancer of the cervix furnishes an excellent illustration of all these difficulties. Screening by cervical smears for abnormal cells was well under way in Canada and the United States in the 1950s. Its benefits have still not been conclusively demonstrated by impeccable trial, but within the past few years the Department of Health has felt ethically bound to introduce such a service here, giving the validity of the method the benefit of the doubt. The situation is certainly one in which effective screening would be expected to yield dividends. Cancer of the cervix is fatal in a high proportion of radically treated patients, and it would probably be very nearly always fatal untreated. Its habit of developing to an advanced stage without symptoms of any kind is notorious. The results of treatment in the early stages are undoubtedly better than in late cases. Furthermore the incidence of clinically detected cancer in British Columbia has fallen by more than half during ten years of screening and early surgery—though this remarkable finding is susceptible to various interpretations in detail. However, if these are the facts, what are the difficulties? The first is that we just don't know the natural history of the condition revealed by the abnormal cell changes detected in the cervical smear. Are the changes spontaneously reversible? Are cases of later clinical cancer recruited essentially from those with positive smears and if so how often, and after how long? After all, somewhat analogous changes are often seen in the male prostate at post-mortem, but prostatic cancer is relatively uncommon clinical disease. These are extremely important questions because a positive cervical smear is increasingly regarded as an indication for either minor or major surgery—and sometimes quite extensive surgery undertaken in an otherwise healthy young woman without a single symptom.

If we accept the informal evidence that cervical screening is almost certainly beneficial it would be reasonable to extend it first to the most vulnerable section of the population—the older, sexually promiscuous members of the lower social classes living in unhygienic circumstances. Here a final difficulty arises: experience confirms that these are also the people least likely to accept the suggestion. Indeed, amongst those who clamour for this and similar forms of examination ardent middle-class church workers are much more conspicuous.

Screening tests for breast cancer are more elaborate and more expensive. They comprise clinical examination, infra-red photography, soft-tissue X-rays to sort out false positives, and in many cases surgical removal of suspicious breast tumours for microscopical examination. Breast cancer is the leading cause of female cancer deaths and is about four times as common as cervical cancer, with a 40 per cent five-year survival rate. Unfortunately the results depend much more on the innate malignancy, rate of growth, and stage of extension of the tumour than on the nature of treatment. Since, other things being equal, patients with smaller growths have in general a better outlook than those with large ones, early diagnosis and operation would almost certainly yield some degree of benefit in return for complex investigation, but we do not know for certain whether this gain would be trivial or material. What is clear is that to extend a national annual service on this scale to the 60 per cent or so of women likely to accept it would require the full-time services of more radiologically trained doctors than are working in the whole of Britain today, together with a small army of radiographers and technicians. The techniques so successfully developed during recent years seem likely to find application chiefly as tools of research and for the selective screening of particularly vulnerable groups of patients, such as those who have already had cancer treated in one breast or who have a strong family history of the disease.

Much the same kind of considerations arise in other areas where screening is proposed. There is for example a great deal of asymptomatic undiagnosed early diabetes in the community, especially in the middle-aged and elderly. But where an abnormal blood sugar curve becomes diabetic is a matter of argument, nor do we yet know how far the patient benefits in the long term from the restrictions of treatment before the disease has become a symptomatic nuisance. The same applies to raised blood pressure: we do not know whether the rigorous treatment of early asymptomatic hypertension prolongs life or not. What we do know from our experience of insurance examinations is that its detection can cause disabling anxiety.

But of course the great enthusiasm of the proponents of population screening is reserved for multiple screening, in which a series of tests carried out at a single visit lays the ghosts of a number of diseases and furnishes a 'health profile'. The activities of the Institute of Directors in this connection are well known, and there is an even more enthusiastic service in California where the subject's birthday celebration is scheduled to include an annual sigmoidoscopy, during which he is impaled on what amounts to an illuminated walking-stick in the cause of visual inspection of the lower bowel. The enthusiast here pictures something less ambitious, regularly extended to the general population. This has in fact been undertaken for one or two weeks each year by the Health Department of Rotherham, where a multiphasic screening clinic has offered all comers tests to seek out disturbances of vision, cardiac and respiratory diseases, and cancer of the breast and uterus. The benefits of this bold and elaborate experiment have proved to be few in relation to the resources consumed, especially in the intensive investigation of 'false positives', where abnormal findings are ultimately found to be either insignificant or inexplicable.

Despite enthusiastic pressure from some sections of the medical profession and the public, it is difficult to believe that population screening represents a more effective and economic deployment of resources than the application of the conventional methods of clinical medicine to patients who present with relevant symptoms.

Medical education

The rapid changes in medicine during the past 25 years have also been reflected in something of a crisis in medical education, which remains unresolved. The central problems have been the difficulties of combining education in scientific biology with the cultivation of the personal and human qualities implicit in the doctor–patient relationship. Neither the traditional apprenticeship system of British medical education nor the theoretical–pedagogic approach of continental Europe has satisfactorily met this need. As for ourselves, the traditional division of medical education into two or three years of preclinical studies chiefly centred round anatomy and physiology, followed by two or three years of completely dissociated clinical training, implicit in the Oxbridge–London axis, is under strong attack. An increasing number of university schools of medicine favour an integrated course in which the students' initial motivation is not dissipated by a solid bonus of so-called 'basic' science (which is not always highly relevant to clinical education) and where clinical instruction is increasingly pervaded by the medical science that plays a steadily increasing part in clinical practice, especially in the modern treatment of serious disease.

Beginning with Johns Hopkins at the end of the last century, and continuing today with Western Reserve and the exciting new Canadian schools, North America has led the way in these new developments, and although the difficulties of achieving change sometimes nurture the suspicion that the only way of really altering the medical curriculum is to establish an entirely new medical school, they continue to exert a powerful influence on the university medical schools of the United Kingdom. It must be said at once that the London situation is different. For many London students the sharp division between preclinical and clinical education is implicit in the geographical relationship with the older universities, while the London medical schools themselves owe much more allegiance to their parent hospitals than to the multidisciplinary world of the university. However the Western Reserve pattern that so many have used as a model is itself under strong attack in the United States. The attack has come especially from two quarters—from physicians whose interest transcends the phenomenology of medicine and extends to its social relations, and from medical students who doubt the relevance of intensive concentration on high scientific technology in trying to cope with the complex medico-social problems of an unstable, inequitable, and fragmented society. Some of the criticisms of modern medical education from such sources are undoubtedly valid. There is an excessive concentration on the hospital as opposed to the community, and on the relatively small amount of serious illness that is treated in institutions at the expense of attention to common causes of disablement. Above all there is an emphasis on the dramatic possibility of cure rather than the continuing problem of care that absorbs an ever-increasing proportion of total resource in an ageing population. On the face of it, it is inherently illogical that medical education should be almost entirely based on the small proportion of patients referred to hospital. But how can a system based on the primary medical consultation be fully integrated with medical science, with its enormous and unequivocal benefits? The scientifically orientated physician or surgeon can point with some justification to the dangers of amateurism. Attempts have been made in several British medical schools to introduce an element of general practice into the curriculum. This was at first resisted by most established teachers and consultants on the grounds that few practitioners knew enough to teach, and indeed there are few schools even today where the time devoted to instruction in family medicine amounts to very much in terms of the course as a whole. On the other hand students themselves have greatly appreciated the opportunity of seeing sickness in the home rather than merely in the hospital, and of learning how the doctor copes with these difficult problems. It is significant that where such courses have been given as an option late in the undergraduate curriculum there have been many enthusiastic takers. Those who oppose expenditure of student time in this way feel that the logistics pertaining to a particular kind of medical practice can be learned best only after graduation.

One of the most interesting attempts to solve this problem has been made in the new Medical School at Calgary. With the development of the oil industry, Alberta has become one of the world's wealthiest communities. It has a first-class medical school of high quality and traditional pattern at Edmonton, but there has been a widespread feeling in Alberta that while it trained excellent specialists and medical scientists of international standard, it did not entirely meet the practical needs of Alberta's very widespread communities. The Calgary school, under the leadership of a team led by a very able young paediatrician, has organized its curriculum around primary medical care. The teaching will be based on what amounts in essence to a large group general-practice clinic on the ground floor of a building that houses the laboratories, library, and teaching space of the medical school in its upper storeys and is adjacent to and physically connected with a major general hospital. The idea of medical education based on truly comprehensive medical care in this way is ingenious and if it proves successful could well set a pattern for the future.

Whether or not curricular innovations prove to be successful they stimulate teachers to re-think their subject and to view it from a different angle. Continuing change of this kind is required by the rapid changes in medicine, and of course they require the development of new kinds of teacher, as in the instance of primary medical care mentioned above. Variety and experiment are vital for effective medical training. The capacity of young people to resist education can hardly be over-estimated, and although the graduates of Harvard, Glasgow, and Oxford may have had remarkably different patterns of education, the best at the age of 30 are virtually indistinguishable, having reached the same standard of professional excellence by quite different routes. The universities and the medical schools must certainly resist the arbitrary imposition of uniform rules for training about which one hears much in the corridors of the Common Market. The independence of British universities and professional bodies will require protection against the pattern so familiar in continental Europe where such bodies are often subservient organs of central government from whom they receive detailed instructions. This situation seems to be accepted in the EEC Commission, and would doubtless have its attractions for our own civil service, but it would be disastrous for medicine, science, and education. In general terms there seems to be wide agreement that the pattern of basic training is best integrated and not divided on an oil-and-water basis into preclinical and clinical segments, and that there must be a basic general qualification followed by more vocationally-orientated postgraduate education, expanded and in some degree formalized. These goals can undoubtedly be reached by various routes. Despite the old pattern of the Oxbridge–London arrangement it trains excellent doctors in every field of medicine. The same goes for the Western Reserve's integrated curriculum, and for the medical education of the Soviet Union, where specialization obtains from the middle of the undergraduate course of instruction. The main difference concerns the time when specialization begins, and there is nothing intrinsically wrong with our existing system of four to six years of basic professional education followed by a three- to ten-year period of postgraduate training.

Neglected areas

Accident services

The Cinderellas of the hospital service also deserve mention. In terms of cost-benefit the provision of an effective accident service furnished by a network of fully equipped centres located in general hospitals and providing a 24-hour service, would pay considerable dividends. After a quarter of a century of goading from the profession there are encouraging signs that such a system is now being slowly created. The delay in implementing a scheme dictated by common sense, effectiveness, and economy has been due to a variety of reasons of which three are outstanding. The first is inadequate funding from the Regional Boards. The second concerns the public, which still cherishes the illusion that the benefits of modern medicine and surgery can be made available at every street corner and considers the hospital authorities' threatened closure of small, unworkable, and sometimes positively dangerous units as evidence of malevolent central interference rather than of a serious attempt to improve the standard of service by effective centralization of facilities and personnel. Finally, the profession has a heavy responsibility in this matter. Far too often the hospital's accident service is hopelessly mixed up with casual out-patients, and lacks both top-level clinical direction and authoritative representation in the hospital's administrative structure. More often than not consultant supervision is part-time or even nominal. The young surgeon may have to devote a few years to such duties on his way up the professional ladder, but there are few even amongst the larger institutions where the problems of trauma are regarded with the respect they deserve, where they are the subject of serious continuing research, and where there is a clear and promising career structure for the surgeon prepared to spend his professional life in this exacting and important field. It is exhausting work for the senior man, but his skills yield a higher recovery rate here than in most other branches of surgery.

Mental subnormality

Attention has recently been drawn to the nature and magnitude of the problem of mental subnormality by a series of scandals involving inadequate care and sometimes actual ill-treatment in several large under-staffed institutions. There are more than 60 000 adults in institutions for the subnormal and more than 100 000 subnormal children and adults living outside them. Retarded children can live at home with their families unless their behaviour is seriously disturbed, in which case they may require supervision in special units: otherwise the need is chiefly for short-term admission for family reasons. The major need is of course for residential accommodation for the subnormal adults whose parents are no longer able to care for them, and this presents a real problem. Not only is the expense of furnishing civilized conditions considerable, but the staffing of such institutions presents special difficulties. Only a minority of nurses and other attendants can rise to the challenge of what is an arduous and not always rewarding task, and recruitment is difficult.

The chance of an overall improvement in national standards of significant degree is remote at the present time, but there are two steps that could be taken to improve the situation. The first of these is the establishment of pilot schemes in selected areas where combinations of different forms of residential and non-residential care and training could be set up and evaluated as the rational basis for an ultimate pattern of services on a national scale; the second is a larger investment in research directed to the prevention of subnormality. This is easily said but more difficult than it sounds. At one end of the scale are the severely subnormal where there is often either a structural abnormality of the nervous system or an identifiable or suspected biochemical abnormality. Such cases are few in number, but can to some extent be prevented by new methods of early diagnosis and selective abortion. The larger number of moderately subnormal patients presents a more difficult problem in that the causal factors of moderate subnormality are little understood. It is here that intensive prospective study using epidemiological and genetic techniques and based on the study of a large series of pregnancies is most likely to yield useful information. In this connection there is something of a vicious circle. The depressed and depressing nature of much work with the mentally subnormal has led to depressed professional recruitment into the field, and a deliberate effort will be required to bring expert investigators from outside into this particular area. Such people are hard to come by and hard to encourage to enter this field, but the establishment of three or four major research units in appropriate university medical centres selected on the basis of the excellence of their infrastructure in neurology, psychiatry, genetics, and biochemistry might be expected to pay long-term dividends. It would seem that there is at least as much chance of reducing the incidence of mental subnormality as of improving the facilities for the care and management of its victims.

The mildly subnormal present of course a quite different problem and are characterized chiefly by poor work records and a tendency to slide into delinquency and petty crime. This is a vast problem which can be dealt with only by social support.

Chronic disease and geriatrics

The third sector of relative neglect in the hospital service concerns the fields of chronic disease and of geriatrics. The problem of the chronic sick is separate from that of geriatrics, which deals with illnesses that are often acute and treatable in the elderly, and with their rehabilitation.

The wide publicity attendant on the splendid work of a small group of specially dedicated clinicians gives grounds for reasonable hope of a steady improvement in the humane and comforting management of terminal illness. It is less easy, alas, to feel confident about the general care of chronic disease and of the elderly. Many of the triumphs of modern curative medicine and surgery transform the victim of an acute and previously fatal illness into a state somewhere between almost normal medicated survival and disastrously protracted invalidism. The degree of invalidism in some patients— those who are steroid-dependent, for example—often makes the physician wish he had never embarked on the initial treatment. Chronic patients suffering from organic or psychiatric illness will remain with us and their numbers are likely to increase. This increase applies even more certainly to the elderly. There must be scarcely a family in the land that does not face the difficult problem of caring for aged relatives, for whom our society is ill equipped to cope. Maiden aunts are a thing of the past, spare rooms are almost as infrequent, and the total adult population is either out at work or wishes it were. The trouble is that this is both a medical and a social problem. Most of these elderly people are neither ill nor well. They do not require elaborate treatment, which in the very old is all too often cruel as well as inappropriate. What they do require is care of the kind that will keep them mobile, semi-independent, and in some sort of stimulating circulation.

By international standards British achievement in the care of the elderly is more than respectable, and we have done a great deal since Marjorie Warren galvanized geriatrics out of the 'chronic sick wards' in the 1930s. Especially since the inception of the NHS we have developed many facilities for the care of the aged and established geriatrics as an important part of internal medicine. Nevertheless, institutional facilities in many parts of the country are grossly inadequate and sometimes not even civilized. And although medical education ought by now to mirror the great importance of the problems of old age in contemporary medicine, the teaching hospitals have been slow to accept responsibility in this field and have especially neglected its educational importance.

In the field of community services the unevenness of local authority provision is truly remarkable. Twenty years after the inauguration of the health service nearly a quarter of our county boroughs had made no special provision for housing the elderly, and nearly half our county councils provided fewer than 50 home helps per 100 000 population. Even where the provision looks good on paper it is often woefully inadequate in operation. There is little continuity in the home-help service and the wait for a hostel place or hospital bed often seems interminable. The contrast with such provision in the Soviet Union is a poor advertisement for western values.

Between 1901 and 1966 there has been a four-fold increase in our total population above the age of 65. The percentage has increased from 5 to 12 per cent. More than half the 'chronic' patients in general practice are over 60, and more than half of all who survive to the age of 70 receive regular medical attention. The majority of old people live at home, many with relatives, but about two million without a near-by relative, a million and a half entirely alone. They make severe demands on domiciliary services: they use more doctor's time, more drugs, and more ancillary services. The 300 000 who live in institutions are divided between NHS hospitals and local authority homes. The 12 per cent of the total population over 65 occupies over a third of all NHS hospital beds; many of those in hospitals would otherwise be living alone.

This present increase in the proportion of the elderly in the population reflects fluctuation in birth-rate early in the century rather than the improved chances of survival in childhood which have operated for the last 30 years. These have yet to be reflected in an anticipated increase in the proportion of the aged during the closing decades of the present century. The problem is therefore inescapable.

The demand for medical care in this connection may be alarming but it is in no way surprising. Except for occasional acute illnesses most of us remain fit until our sixties, and it would be a ridiculous disposition of medical resources that denied them to the age-group that stands in most need. The drama of the situation is sometimes exaggerated. The number of elderly people abandoned by their families is small, and many of those who live proudly independent existences do so voluntarily and in spite of pressure from their families. But it is beyond question the socially isolated who make special demands on medical services, and under present circumstances many of their needs are inadequately met.

It is important to grasp the difference between the care of the chronic sick and that of the aged. Good geriatric medicine is in the first instance concerned with early, accurate, and expert diagnosis of illnesses of the elderly which are often acute or subacute, and its function is to forestall and prevent their development into chronic incapacity. Geriatrics is the preventive as well as the clinical medicine of old age. A good example is the frequency with which subacute mental confusion or atypical depressive syndromes in the elderly arise from intercurrent but clinically inconspicuous physical illness and are rapidly reversible with effective treatment of such conditions as urinary or pulmonary infection, mild uraemia from prostatic enlargement, cardiac infarction, thyroid deficiency, or pernicious anaemia.

Before returning to the care of the elderly, however, let us just for a moment consider the separate problem of the chronic sick. This is primarily a problem of logistics, and it is seen in its most classical form in my own field of neurology. In the context of the teaching or special hospital the patient with organic disease of the nervous system referred to a neurological physician remains under his supervision so long as expert treatment is required. In the case of epilepsy or myasthenia gravis this may be for life—unless the epilepsy is so severe as to require institutional care, underlining the paradox that the expert must often decant the severest cases. But if forms of treatment specifically regarded as the province of the neurologist are no longer applicable—as in the case of brain tumour after operation or chronic multiple sclerosis—the patient more often than not passes from the specialist's orbit either to a back room at home or to a miscellaneous ward for chronic sick in an ex-workhouse. This happens not because the neurologist wants to disavow responsibility for the chronic case—he knows he could learn much from studying the later as well as the earlier phases of organic nervous diseases, to say nothing of the salutary lessons to be learned from ultimate post-mortem examination—but because of the way our hospitals are organised. General hospials still bear the stamp of their nineteenth-century voluntary origin and fight shy of responsibility for chronic illness.

This is far too often hidden away from the public, the medical student, and the specialist and left in hands that are sometimes devoted but not always highly skilled. And if necropsy is performed it will more often than not be undertaken as a routine chore by a run-of-the-mill pathologist with no special interest in the case and no informed clinician to jog his elbow and learn and teach the lessons on which progress in clinical medicine depends. In this respect we are far behind many of our colleagues on the continent of Europe, where neurologists are often in a position to emulate the example of Charcot in following his personal cases over the years and ultimately to the post-mortem room. The care of patients with chronic disease will be significantly improved only when they remain under the general supervision of the appropriate specialist throughout their illnesses. The corollary of this arrangement is that every major general hospital must have its own chronic wing manned by its regular staff.

With regard to geriatrics, there is of course an overall shortage of geriatric beds. Some districts have less than one bed per thousand of the population, and few have two. There has been little operational research within the health service into the number of beds needed in a community, to say nothing of the requirements of populations with different social circumstances and age distributions. There have been estimates that if community supportive services were adequate, ten beds per thousand people aged over 65 would probably meet present needs—except where the social environment was especially unfavourable. Needless to say, local provision should also take future population trends into account.

Few regions meet the bed requirements and none furnishes effective and adequate community services. With regard to staffing at every level, geriatrics is one of the Cinderellas of the service. One department known to me seems to run 630 beds on one consultant, one registrar, one-and-a-half senior house officers, and some GP help. In the nursing field the myth also dies hard that geriatric departments can get by with fewer nurses than medical or surgical units. In fact they need a higher ratio of nurses both in the acute and rehabilitation wards, though in the latter auxiliaries can play a prominent and valuable part.

One point that must be remembered is that although centralization pays dividends in providing highly specialized facilities, it is less applicable in the care of the elderly, where services must be built into the community served. Although small units tend to be expensive, some degree of decentralization taps useful sources of staff recruitment that might otherwise remain unused and encourages voluntary helpers whose work with the aged is invaluable.

New buildings for geriatrics are unlikely to be made available on anything like the scale required. Fortunately, there are many elderly but not absolutely impossible hospitals up and down the country, and especially in densely populated areas, that can be adapted and cheerfully refurbished to meet the need.

A comprehensive geriatric service needs several types of hospital accommodation. Acute illnesses require all the facilities of a general medical ward or a similarly equipped geriatric diagnostic and assessment unit. The main function of specifically geriatric wards should be active rehabilitation. Between these two there is room for an intermediate type of accommodation used for convalescence —for patients needing intermittent hospital care or a place to stay while their families enjoy a holiday.

Another form of accommodation needed is the day hospital, which is a cheap, valuable, and insufficiently developed concept limited by transport provision, which is rarely adequate. Some long-term beds are also needed for patients who cannot be rehabilitated. Increasingly these comprise the demented who block beds at every level, who cannot be managed at home, and whose growing number threatens to swamp every department of the district general hospitals. This very serious situation can be met only by collaboration between geriatricians, psychiatrists, and directors of social services, all of whom must have increased resources. In this context the Seebohm dissociation of health from welfare is proving absolutely disastrous.

If a humane and effective service is to be provided, all these facilities should be under the control of a team led by consultant geriatricians, and, as in the case of chronic illness at other ages, intractable cases should not be passed down the line to a lower level of care, as happens in some parts of the world. Furthermore, geriatrics is predominantly the general medicine of a particular but large age-group and should be an integral part of it. It is absolutely essential that the geriatrician should first be a good physician, able to take his place in the medical team, able to share in the care of patients in other age-groups, and standing in for his general medical colleagues when need be. Where this is recognized and acted upon, the best geriatric care flourishes and recruitment to the specialty presents fewest problems.

But the problem is, of course, complex and goes far beyond the provision of hospital care. It would certainly not be solved by a *pro rata* rise in bed numbers to parallel the projected increase in the elderly population at risk. Community care is all-important and its provision is less adequate and more uneven than that of hospital facilities. In this connection the local authorities' performance has been generally poor. Few even approach recommended norms—which are none too high. Already the hospitals can rehabilitate more of the elderly than the social services can reintegrate into the community.

The geriatric hospital discharge rate and bed turnover depend on two main factors: the level of staffing of the unit and the adequacy of neighbourhood community services. Few areas furnish welfare homes for the frail but otherwise healthy aged, and fewer still provide enough of the inconspicuously supervised housing now regarded as preferable for many such cases. The same applies to the economic provision of day hospitals. In all these connections the historical dichotomy between health and welfare services has inhibited the development of an effectively integrated service and local authorities have mostly failed to fulfil their responsibilities, some of them frankly admitting that they are unwilling to spend ratepayers' money to relieve pressure on the centrally funded hospital service.

If close integration of geriatric and general medical staff is vital to the effective functioning of the hospital side of the service, similar integration between the community doctor and the hospital is equally essential to maintain the tenuous link between the two branches of the service. The continued illogical and artificial division between health and welfare maintained in the latest proposals for reorganization of the health service will consolidate the present unsatisfactory situation and ensure that collaboration continues to encounter considerable practical difficulties.

There are many other ways apart from welfare homes and day hospitals in which community services are vital but generally inadequate. Many old people who genuinely require medical attention can never bring themselves to request it and the help of local authority social workers is indispensable to the GP in the case-finding activities that represent first-line medicine in this context. Active case-finding is imperative if the facilities provided are to be effectively used and if tragedies are to be averted. An adequate home help service would in itself reduce the number of demands for urgent admission to hospital which constitute so large a part of geriatric practice and could largely be avoided by an organized continuing service. Such simple things as a shopping service, a telephone for the elderly living alone, and transport provision to attend day hospitals or out-patient clinics would in themselves prolong the economic solution of independent existence at home for many borderline cases. The same applies in the case of mobile meal services, laundry facilities, and the provision of community physicians with a special responsibility and interest in the care of the elderly.

Local authorities are not merely slow to fulfil their obligations to furnish reasonable standards in these connections but, by the standards of the hospital service, their machinery is unthinkably slow and cumbersome. Local authorities have, for example, a statutory obligation to make minor alterations to the houses of disabled people to enable them to obtain access by wheelchair. Within my own clinical experience interminable delays involved in undertaking such work have led to prolonged and unnecessary retention in hospital and finally to the patient paying from his own pocket to have the work done quickly.

Psychogeriatrics presents a special and increasing problem. Delirium, depression, and dementia account for 95 per cent of patients in this field. Two of the three are eminently curable. Many acute psychiatric episodes can be as adequately treated in a geriatric ward as in a medical ward. Psychiatry is too serious a subject and psychiatric illnesses are too common to be left entirely to psychiatrists. Every geriatrician, like every physician, should be expected to have some clinical ability in this field just as in cardiac or respiratory disease.

There is also room in each area for a psychiatrist with a special interest in the mental disorders of the elderly to hold a joint appointment in psychiatry and geriatrics with responsibilities in both mental and geriatric hospitals. A few forward-looking authorities have already developed psychogeriatric day hospitals and these may play a valuable part in permitting the load of mental illness in the elderly to be shared between the family and the community. The present fashion for the early discharge of psychotic patients back to their families has the blessing of central authority and makes a contribution to the favourable showing of mental hospitals in terms of turnover and recovery rate. But the geriatrician, who is less institution-bound and more closely linked with the patient's home, is often better able than the psychiatrist to appreciate the impact of such discharge on the patient's family and the immeasurable but very real economic and emotional disturbance it may occasion to a wide circle. Collaboration between the two specialties should teach the psychiatrist the lessons that geriatrics has learned in the matter of flexibility—the value, for example, of periods spent in hospital, at home, or in attendance at a day hospital, for the mildly demented patient, rather than the orthodox long-term institutionalization which is more likely to suggest itself to physicians working in the milieu of a large mental hospital.

Dental health
The facts about British dental health certainly qualify it as another neglected area of the health service. They are frankly appalling, by comparison, for example, with the situation in North America or Scandinavia. Eighty per cent of our five-year-olds already have some decayed, missing or (rarely) filled teeth. Half our

population has lost all its natural teeth by middle age. Our dentists extract ten million decayed teeth every year and carry out nearly thirty million fillings. A quarter of our young people need dentures by the time they are twenty. All these figures reflect of course the incidence of dental caries. But the statistics with regard to disease of the gums and periodontal tissue are if anything even more depressing. Less than 20 per cent of any random sample of the adult population have reasonably healthy gums. This pandemic oral ill-health, unfavourably noted by every physician who comes from overseas to work in our hospitals, is accepted by the public with a complacency that will strike subsequent generations as astonishing, because of course it is largely preventable. One is tempted to echo Edward the Seventh's famous remark made at Midhurst about tuberculosis: 'If preventable, why not prevented?'

The cause of dental caries is multifactorial. The genetic factor is significant but difficult to identify. Much the same applies to the effect of maternal illness and nutrition during pregnancy. When we come to consider early illness in the infant or young child we are on firmer ground, and there can be little doubt that this is one factor in determining susceptibility to caries. As often, however, medicine is stronger on pathogenesis (the mechanism of disease production) than aetiology (primary causation). There is fairly general agreement that caries is due to bacterial fermentation of sticky carbohydrates on and between the teeth, which produces an acid that destroys the enamel surface of the teeth and ultimately penetrates to the softer dentine and eventually the pulp. In other words dental decay is the price the public pays for eating more than half a million tons of sweets each year. Although brushing the teeth helps to prevent infection of the gums it has little effect in preventing or reducing decay. In other words, and contrary to popular belief, brushing the teeth is at least as important to the middle-aged as to the child. Although the possibility of killing or inhibiting micro-organisms on the teeth by brushing with special antiseptics or of inoculating with vaccine derived from the micro-organisms mainly responsible may at some time in the future enable us to prevent dental caries, there can be no doubt whatever that the most effective method of prevention at present is fluoridation of the water supply. The addition of one part of fluoride to a million of water has a remarkable and fully confirmed effect in diminishing its prevalence. There are certain parts of the country where this concentration has occurred naturally and for many years, and there is no shred of evidence that it has had any ill-effects, and plenty of evidence that the incorporation of fluoride in the dental enamel is associated with a much reduced incidence of dental decay.

There can be no doubt that fluoridation of the water supply is the simplest and most effective prophylactic measure. Objections to fluoridation are insubstantial and ill-informed, quoting levels of administration far in excess of anything envisaged, and the children amongst the three million people in Britain whose water is already treated in this way are fortunate.

One interesting development in preventive dentistry is the application of fluoride directly to the teeth three times a year by a dental hygienist, with reduction in subsequent decay and in the need for later reparative dental treatment. Here, however, we encounter one of the major anomalies of the situation in British dentistry. There is no provision whatever for preventive dentistry under the NHS. To understand this it is necessary to look back briefly at the history of the service.

When Aneurin Bevan introduced the health service he had to make compromises to obtain the reluctant support of the medical profession. One of them was of course the sharp division between hospital and general practice which survives to the present day and which even Sir Keith Joseph's latest White Paper does not successfully bridge. However, probably because of their long experience of the panel system, Mr. Bevan was able to obtain the agreement of the doctors to contract for the comprehensive medical care of their patients. With a very few exceptions the care extended is in fact comprehensive, and there is no extra charge for any special kind of attention required. The dentists, however, opted for a system essentially based on piecework. It is extremely elaborate and makes no provision whatever for preventive dentistry, being essentially a repair and casualty service and even at this level grossly inadequate. We have less than 12 000 dentists in general Health Service practice today, and in ten years the total number of new registrations has increased by less than 2000. Scandinavia has more than twice as many in relation to population. Our practitioners are grossly overworked and the system encourages fast work and the use of the cheapest materials available. One recent survey showed that the average time spent by British dentists in providing full upper and lower dentures is 70 minutes, as compared with an average of 170 minutes for a consultant dental surgeon working in hospital here and no less than 300 minutes in practice in Canada. More than 95 per cent of partial dentures supplied in 1968 had a plastic base rather than the more expensive and much more durable metal base. The present fee for full dentures under the NHS is £16.50. The fee for a similar service under the Social Health Insurance Service in Germany is about £120. The German technician in fact receives more than twice as much as the total fee of the British dentist and his technician combined, for the same service.

One of the most alarming features of this situation is the low morale of the profession, and especially that part of it concerned with dental education. The training is thorough and scientific as regards the technical aspects of the profession, though in the context of British practice it is not surprising that preventive dentistry receives less emphasis. But the students are taught techniques that they will probably have little opportunity of practising once they leave the dental school. Delicate crown and bridge work which can so often obviate the need for the inconvenience of dentures is virtually impracticable under NHS conditions and terms of practice, and requires special justification before being authorized by the Dental Estimates Board.

What is being done about this? The answer is very little indeed. A powerful committee under Lord Teviot studied the problem from 1943 to 1946 and made excellent recommendations. After careful study of need it estimated, for example, that at least 20 000 active dental practitioners were required to furnish an adequate service: 25 000 would be the minimum present-day equivalent. The Teviot Report also emphasized the need for an extensive programme of research and prevention and the urgent replacement of many obsolete dental schools. The snail's pace of progress in all these directions is eloquent testimony to the lowly position the dental services have occupied in the priority list of a succession of responsible Ministers. Except in Scotland preventive dentistry has hardly got off the ground. The financial basis of professional remuneration might have been specifically designed to produce a cheap and nasty service. It also ensures that since dental surgery is arduous and physically as well as mentally exhausting, this is the only profession where for the majority of practitioners earnings decline progressively after middle-age. It may be that the government would like to opt out of the dental side of the NHS except for especially vulnerable members of the population, and leave the whole thing to private practice. This view would probably obtain support within a profession of which many members regard salaried service as anathema. However with a very inadequate number of dentists in the community, with no realistic steps to increase the output of graduates, and with a steady and inevitable increase in the need for dental attention contingent on the change in the age distribution of the population, such a step could only make matters worse. Few would be able to afford the high real costs of first-class private dentistry, and for the most part these would in all probability be those least likely to stand in need of it. The position is serious. It is tempting to suggest a Royal Commission, but the fate of the Teviot Report (1946) and of the McNair (1956) proposals for dental health education gives grounds for little hope that its report would do other than gather dust on a shelf in the Department of Health and Social Services.

3

Some ethical considerations

Medical ethics have in the past been mainly concerned with such everyday affairs as protecting the patient from negligence or assault and preventing the doctor from advertising the special quality of his skills or from sleeping with his patients. However, more sophisticated ethical considerations are inseparable from many of the issues of priority that have already been discussed. The development of introspective attitudes in the medical profession on these subjects is a new phenomenon but it is not surprising. It is only since modern scientific medicine furnished radical opportunities to influence the course of serious disease that the profession has been faced with such difficult choices as to treat or not to treat. Until thirty years ago opportunities to cure diseases as opposed to relieving symptoms were few and far between. But the accelerating pace of medical progress has brought with it new complications. The simple Hippocratic rule of preserving life at all costs and at all times is no longer in itself an adequate guide to the humane and civilized practice of medicine. Not only is the doctor forced to consider the quality of survival that his treatment will produce, but also its possible implications for society. Indeed, there are a number of sensitive areas in which the possibility clearly arises of conflict between the interests of the individual patient and those of the society of which he is a member. Such problems are raised for example by the possible effects of the treatment of hereditary disease on the frequency of unfavourable genes in the population, the maintenance of the helpless idiot, intensive therapy, surgery for spina bifida, the care of the aged population, and the social management of seriously psychopathic behaviour.

Some ethical considerations

Genetics

Modern contraceptive techniques, advancing knowledge of human genetics, the increasing availability of genetic counselling services, and the possibility of eliminating abnormal foetuses by selective abortion based on cytological and biochemical examination of amniotic fluid have brought planned parenthood and the avoidance of some genetic disasters within general reach. However there are very real difficulties, quite apart from the simple one of improving the reliability of such facilities and making them generally available. It is unlikely that any democratic society will delegate the responsibility for final personal decisions in these matters from the parents. And the trouble is of course that the parents from whom difficult decisions are most likely to be required are all too often drawn from the most feckless and irresponsible section of the population. The problematical issue of a positive as opposed to a negative eugenic policy (breeding for favourable genes rather than for the elimination of unfavourable ones) is fatally complicated by the fact that, unlike the breeders of horses for courses, we don't and can't really know exactly what we want: the qualities desirable in a 1918 infantryman are not necessarily those appropriate to an astronaut.

But the general problem is inescapable. Before the discovery of insulin in 1921 juvenile diabetes was invariably fatal. Today the juvenile diabetic survives to reproductive age. The pool of un-favourable genes is steadily increased and with it the incidence of diabetic blindness and kidney failure. This underlines the dilemma: it would be unthinkable to deny treatment to the young diabetic but its ultimate implications for society cannot but be unfavourable. Curiously geneticists, with a different time-scale, are less disturbed by such developments than physicians, who face their clinical implications in day-to-day practice.

The effective treatment of patients with certain hereditary bio-chemical disorders of the brain, and of the pre-cancerous condition of multiple small tumours in the large bowel are similar examples of this dilemma. The individual patient's health can be restored and preserved, in the first instance by life-long drug treatment, and in the second by surgical operation, but the inescapable price of therapeutic success is the wider distribution of unfavourable genes in the population. Again the geneticists are much less alarmed by this than the physicians, since they consider the likely rate of multiplication of the unfavourable genes in the case of these rather rare disorders slow enough to be inconsiderable. This certainly applies to recessive conditions and is possibly also true for the large number of diseases where heredity is no more than one of a number of factors involved in the genesis of the disease. However, effective treatment for a dominant disorder is likely to double its frequency amongst all live births within one generation. There are few patients with each condition, but there are many such conditions, and the prospect is unattractive.

A rather different problem is raised by schizophrenia. Of this about all that can be said is that a hereditary factor is certainly important, whether it is unitary or multi-factorial. Schizophrenics previously had a low rate of fertility, but successful drug treatment has led to many more of them being able to live in the community, and a movement of schizophrenic fertility towards the normal is already clearly evident. Schizophrenia affects 1 per cent of the total population and whatever the exact nature of its genetic basis, successful treatment seems bound to lead to an increase in its frequency in the community, though the incidence could take anything from seven to twenty generations to double.

To the writer it seems that Huntington's chorea is a touchstone of society's attitude to such problems. This disease is world-wide, and characterized by persistent twitching and remorseless mental deterioration. It is inherited as a dominant characteristic, and since it usually becomes clinically evident only during adult life it is self-perpetuating. In the seventeenth century it was regarded by Cotton Mather as a manifestation of witchcraft: clinically it was recognized as a familial disease-entity by George Huntington on Long Island in 1872. Although its downhill course occasionally shows inexplicable fluctuations it is so far as we know virtually unaffected by environmental factors. Its adult onset means that opportunities for reproduction are almost universal, and the members of such families who are prepared to accept advice about the unwisdom of reproduction are few. Most feel themselves likely to escape the taint, and concealment of the family history is very common. For this reason the scourge continues generation after generation. It seems as unlikely that clinically unaffected members of such families will accept voluntary sterilization as that society will impose it on a compulsory basis, and if this is so the disease seems likely to be with us indefinitely. In these circumstances pleas for voluntary restraint in other diseases where heredity is less definitely involved have a hollow ring, and discussion of compulsory sterilization is likely to be pejoratively dismissed as tantamount to Nazism. The impatient biologist can only console himself with the reflection that society is political rather than rational, and the physician is unlikely to be greatly reassured by the clinical geneticist's optimism as to the anticipated long-term efficacy of genetic counselling.

It is of course possible to alter the genetic pattern of the chromosome by various crude manipulations such as radiation and experimental virus infection. But despite the current enthusiasm of 'genetic engineers' the possibility of deliberately changing the heritable genetic endowment of the individual human being is at present beyond our grasp, perhaps fortunately.

Keeping people alive

The problem of keeping people alive is one that would have seemed unreal to any physician a quarter of a century ago, since his efforts were directed against all odds to maintaining life for as long as possible, irrespective of all other considerations. The problem has been vividly raised by the success of the anaesthaesiologist in sustaining the vital functions of fatally damaged patients for periods of weeks or even months by assisted respiration. The spectacular success of intensive care units—for example in controlling the terrifying failure of respiration that occurs in some acute and entirely recoverable diseases of the nervous system, or in keeping patients alive with severe but recoverable head injury—has served to highlight the effectiveness of these methods. In the same way they may be employed where the patient is a victim of a desperately serious but obscure disease in order to buy time for definitive diagnosis or to maintain life for as long as possible when the outcome remains open to doubt, as in some cases of poisoning. Intensive care can however be misused. It is clearly pointless to keep a patient with an inoperable brain tumour breathing when a fatal outcome is certain, and in the case of recurrent chest infections in the elderly respiratory cripple there may come a time when it is unkind to rescue the patient yet again from an acute episode only to restore him to distressing permanent disablement. The decision to submit a patient to resuscitation or intensive therapy must be informed, deliberate, and responsible. When damage is clearly irrecoverable the physician must steel himself not to prolong life artificially beyond the point at which the patient's interests are served. Assisted respiration of a severely head-injured patient may furnish time for definitive assessment by X-rays or surgical exploration, and if this reveals physical brain damage so gross that it precludes survival the doctor must overcome his reluctance to disconnect the respirator. This lesson has now been learned, though it is one reason why work in an intensive care unit is more than averagely exacting and harrowing.

One purpose of units of this kind was to concentrate scarce and expensive nursing and medical care and its accompanying technology in areas where it was most needed. Appropriate patients are usually admitted to an intensive care unit for a fairly short period of time, before being moved or returned to general ward accommodation in the event of survival.

This is a field where anything in the way of truly controlled therapeutic trial presents extraordinary practical and ethical difficulties. Its high cost in relation to other medical needs must be borne in mind. The total cost of a bed in an intensive care unit can be as much as £450 per week. In other words a ten-bedded unit costs nearly £250 000 a year to run, and it has been estimated that of about 500 admissions 50 lives are saved annually at a cost approaching £5000 per case. Such astronomical costs naturally raise the question as to whether it is ethical to concentrate so much resource on so small a number of patients when there are many neglected areas of medical care. Needless to say most of us would hope that such facilities might be available for ourselves and our families if need be. But there are other and more important considerations. The first is that the scrupulous attention to detail in the intensive care unit influences the general standards of nursing and medical care throughout the hospital; the second, that it affords opportunity for experimental trial and technical improvement which end in simplification and general availability of methods that were at first esoteric. These units have proved their value in the large and already well-equipped centres that can support them, and have exerted a profound influence over the past five years on the general standard of care of the gravely ill and especially the unconscious patient. It is in such cases that the method finds its most effective application. However, even with stringent selection of cases and scrupulous care of patients there are bound to be a certain number in whom the quality of survival indicates that the attempt was ill-fated. The most spectacular instances concern very serious head injury, where assisted respiration is thoroughly justified by the unpredictability of the outcome and the continuing off-chance of recovery but where in the event a miserable vegetable existence is prolonged for many months to no purpose. This raises in an acute form the whole question of the quality of survival, a topic that is most clearly illustrated by a consideration of the treatment of congenital anomalies and especially spina bifida.

Spina bifida

The preservation of the gravely handicapped patient is a more circumscribed problem, but since it is often a direct consequence of deliberate elective medical interference it is the subject of serious anxiety within the profession. Most infections, acute gastro-intestinal diseases, and nutritional disorders have been brought under fairly complete control in the developed countries. Paediatric research today concentrates its attention on what was formerly regarded as nature's wastage—on the investigation and treatment of congenital defects and genetic faults. Recent developments in these fields have raised problems that did not come within Hippocrates' purview, though his contemporaries sanctioned deliberate infanticide for the deformed or weedy infant, and his surgical colleagues did not enthusiastically offer surgical relief for the new-born infant with congenital obstruction of the bowel or gullet, or charge him with the supervision of the uncomprehending child with congenital heart disease, whose life of crippling disability must often be punctuated by the ordeal of repeated major operations.

Paediatrics presents many such problems. Some of these are truly alarming, like retinoblastoma, an inherited cancer of the eye previously 100 per cent fatal but now with a 70 per cent survival rate and fairly certain to be handed on to an increasing population of the descendants of those who have been 'cured' of the disease but not of the genetic anomaly. Or cystic fibrosis, a widespread inherited structural disorder where inevitable death in infancy can now be exchanged for survival as a respiratory cripple. Or severe prematurity—when the triumphant outcome of sophisticated incubation is at considerable risk of serious mental subnormality. Is this, as one of the greatest contemporary American paediatricians has suggested, 'a kind of luxury medicine', using Hippocratic precedent in order that the surgeon's or the paediatrician's prestige and comfort may outweigh a sober assessment of the treatment's real value to the patient in terms of the quality of survival?

These are difficult problems to which there are no easy answers. But a recent meeting of the British Paediatric Association has at any rate gone some way to clarifying one important issue of this kind—the problem of the management of spina bifida. This condition arises from incomplete fusion of the bony spinal column, leaving a defect or an actual hole, usually in the lower part. Minimal degrees of this defect are common and unimportant. Where the defect is rather more severe but the spinal cord and nerve roots are unaffected the condition can often be cured by early surgery. But in many of the more severe cases the bony defect is accompanied by abnormalities in the nerve roots, the spinal cords, and the brain itself. Paralysis of the limbs may be evident at birth, and although even in these cases the gap in the tissues can often be repaired by skilful surgery, hydrocephalus and mental deterioration may be added to the burdens of paralysis and incontinence.

Without operation only about 20 per cent of infants with severe spina bifida survive, and this survival rate requires the provision of two special school places per thousand live births. A careful epidemiological study carried out in Birmingham suggested that operation on all viable infants would treble the number of disabled survivors and raise the demand for special school places to seven per thousand births. Even the earliest and most expert surgery offers a prospect of normal survival to very few severely affected infants. Most uncommitted surgeons have operated only on affected children without paralysis, a general policy which would probably halve the number of surviving disabled children and reduce the demand for special school places to about one per thousand births.

In most centres the policy has been to embark on surgical treatment only where there seems to be a reasonable chance of survival without grave disablement. The trouble is that the decision to operate or not to operate must be made very soon after birth, when assessment of the chances is not easy, especially in borderline cases, and when the surgeon called in by a paediatrician may feel under some sort of moral obligation to undertake surgical interference.

Twelve years ago a group of dedicated and expert paediatricians in Sheffield deliberately decided to admit and treat *all* cases of meningomyelocele, or spina bifida where the spinal cord is present in the sac that protrudes at the site of the bony defect. Between 1959 and 1969 nearly 1200 infants were treated of whom more than 80 per cent were admitted within 24 hours of birth. This bold policy was pursued with whole-hearted enthusiasm. Needless to say it encountered criticism, especially since it made formidable demands on hospital resources in the acute phase and on rehabilitation, institutional provision, and welfare services for the survivors.

The results of this massive experiment are the most favourable that have ever been recorded. They are however profoundly disappointing, and support the critical and conservative approach to treatment rather than that of the enthusiastic interventionist. They go far in fact to confirm the prediction of the Birmingham epidemiologists. Careful follow-up studies show that less than 10 per cent of those originally admitted escaped severe crippling. Two out of every five survivors are mentally retarded, and four have no bladder control. Many have required multiple operations, sometimes as many as a dozen, and many have also suffered distressing complications, amongst which infections of the urinary tract and of the brain itself are conspicuous. Cases with paralysis of the legs, increased circumference of the head, marked deformity of the bony spinal column, severe prematurity, or unfavourable social circumstances seldom benefit from radical treatment. The implications of these findings for the infants, for their families, and for society are disturbing. Indeed if all the cases in the country were treated in this way we would soon have 10 000 such crippled children alive and would ultimately have to support between 20 000 and 30 000 crippled adults in the community. Such socio-economic problems should not in themselves decide the issue, but it is also clear from this important experiment that the interests of the patient with a severe lesion are not served by surgery which can mean only a life of surgical misery and severe residual handicap. The only bright spot in this gloomy story is that the excellence of the clinical study has gone far to define the line beyond which active intervention is unlikely to be helpful, and to allow the surgeon to concentrate in future on the intensive treatment of those less severely afflicted patients in whom it can significantly reduce the final handicap.

Abortion

Liberalization of the law on abortion is an almost world-wide phenomenon, though its pace varies from country to country. It affords reassuring evidence that even the most rigid social attitudes are not entirely insusceptible to reasoned argument and change. The demands for termination of 'accidental' pregnancies will of course decline once effective contraceptive advice is freely and generally available, as it soon must be, but human carelessness and sheer bad luck will determine a certain residual requirement. The position in Britain before the passage of the Abortion Act of 1967 was profoundly unsatisfactory. Many abortions which were entirely justifiable on medical grounds were not carried out for a variety of reasons, including professional prejudice and fear of legal consequences, while abortion on request was fairly widely available both to the patrons of back-street abortionists and to the better-off, who could usually find a compliant gynaecologist. Although the present situation is the subject of a rearguard action, especially by a group of Catholics and self-appointed 'guardians of the unborn child', it presents an enormous improvement. No doubt the steady move towards abortion on request owes a good deal to increasing recognition of the pressure of population increase, but the initial breakthrough which has had social repercussions far outside the United Kingdom, was made by a few enlightened and outstanding lawyers, a group of concerned laymen, and a regrettably small number of doctors—including a handful of intrepid gynaecologists. Numerous red herrings have been trailed across the track, including the demand for beds (very much less than if the pregnancies were allowed to go to term), the expense (trivial by comparison with the cost of an unwanted child in care), the danger of the operation (significantly less than normal delivery following full-term pregnancy), the awful effect on nurses of witnessing termination of pregnancy (in my experience entirely negligible), and the dire psychiatric consequences (which clinical practice confirms as practically always less dire than those of its refusal). Despite the persistence of Mr. St. John-Stevas and whatever the findings of the Lane Committee, it is unthinkable that public opinion will allow the clock to be put back, especially since the operation has been simplified to a point where it can easily and safely be undertaken on an outpatient basis—until the 'morning-after' pill becomes a reality.

Some ethical considerations

Euthanasia

Curiously, euthanasia seems to excite more enthusiasm amongst members of the clergy and the House of Lords than amongst doctors. It is difficult to see any convincing reason why a very ill or decrepit patient should not be allowed to opt to have his life ended, but experience confirms an almost invariable tendency to cling to life even against all odds, and suggests that a deliberate wish of this kind is very exceptional unless mental illness is present, in which case the patient's judgement can hardly be accepted at its face value. What is much more important is to improve the comfort of dying, and there can be no doubt that much remains to be done in this connection especially by the more liberal use of tranquillizers, analgesics, and euphoriants. There are very few clinical situations in which even the most severe pain cannot be controlled during the patient's last days or weeks provided he is in hospital in the charge of a good nurse with a free hand. I have never knowingly terminated a patient's life and I have often had the experience, common to most physicians, of observing remarkable clinical improvement, as well as striking relief of pain and distress, in patients with terminal illness given heroin in dosage that is enormous by conventional standards. There are very occasional cases, such as those of advanced necrotic pelvic cancer which is unbearable to the patient and to those around her, where the administration of a massive dose of intravenous analgesic may be marginally justifiable, but they are very exceptional cases and could not reasonably be used as a basis for a change in the law. In any case the involvement of physicians in euthanasia is surely inadvisable; any step that leaves the patient in doubt as to whether his doctor has come to administer treatment or a quietus would irreparably damage the doctor–patient relationship. It might be more appropriate for an enthusiastic prelate to conduct the patient to the Elysian fields.

Organ transplantation

The operative technique of transplant of live organs was developed 60 years ago, but its general application has been delayed by the inconvenient phenomenon of graft rejection. The first breakthrough came 15 years ago with the demonstration of a high success rate in kidney grafting between identical twins. These favourable results encouraged the extended use of new drugs to suppress the immunological mechanisms by which the body reacts against foreign material introduced into it. Since chronic renal failure is invariably fatal there was nothing to lose from such experimentation. In the event the results were very much better than had been hoped, with 50 per cent two-year survival after cadaver kidney grafts, rising to nearly 80 per cent when the graft came from a close member of the recipient's family. Kidney grafting was made possible by the development of haemodialysis (the artificial kidney) which allowed the maintenance of the patient's life until the operation was feasible. It is largely the absence of methods of compensating for the functions of other diseased organs by such means that delays the large-scale development of other forms of organ grafting. Although the real cost of a kidney transplant has been estimated at somewhere in the region of £5000, the exercise is not uneconomic since the patients are often young and otherwise active and healthy. Most of them can return to a fairly normal life and such survival has already been maintained for more than ten years. The main practical problem is shortage of kidneys for transplantation, which means that the operation is at present made available to rather less than 10 per cent of the 2000 to 3000 patients in Britain who could benefit by it.

The ethical problems of renal transplantation have raised a great deal of controversy, but this is now to a considerable extent overshadowed by the practical problem referred to above. The fear that the treatment of a potential kidney donor might be jeopardized by anxiety to obtain a graft has been largely dispelled by firm professional insistence that the transplant surgeon enters the scene only when the physician or surgeon in charge of the patient is absolutely satisfied that no more can be done. Metaphysical considerations about the moment of death have given place to the formulation of strict standards of the diagnosis of death, aiming to remove a common but unfounded fear that organs might be removed from a patient still alive. Most donor patients have suffered brain damage and show an absence of spontaneous breathing, fixed dilated pupils, the disappearance of deep reflexes, a flat EEG tracing, and radiological or operative evidence of gross structural brain damage. The last is important because there are very rare cases where the first four criteria are fulfilled, especially in severe poisoning, but where recovery is still a possibility. The main problems arise with the so-called 'living corpse', where life is artificially maintained on the respirator, perhaps for a length of time which renders the potential graft useless.

The shortage of kidneys for transplantation is tragic for the sufferers of chronic renal failure, and it is to be hoped that legislation will soon permit the removal of organs for transplantation in a routine manner, as with general post-mortem examination, except where unwillingness has been recorded.

The use of live donors, usually close relatives, has raised even stronger objections than transplantation of kidneys from cadavers, especially by psychiatrists. They fear that moral blackmail might be employed to persuade the relative to donate one of his kidneys rather than see a brother or a sister succumb to renal disease. These fears may not be entirely illusory, though they should be assuaged by tactful handling of the clinical situation, with the maximum of explanation and a minimum of persuasion. To a healthy donor the loss of a single kidney has a very small effect on life expectation, and when one considers the lengths to which rescuers will go in other situations to save a human life, some psychological scruples seem disproportionate.

Renal transplantation is likely to be followed by an extension of the principle to other organs as technical problems are gradually overcome. These concern the typing of tissues for transplant compatibility, arrangements for the expeditious distribution of suitable organs for transplant through a centralized computerized information bank, developments in the preservation of organs, and safer immuno-suppressive treatment. The sensationalism that characterized cardiac transplantation especially is unlikely to be repeated as transplant surgery becomes part of the stock-in-trade of most major surgical units, even though its employment is likely to remain limited to a fairly small group of patients.

Psychopathy

Psychopathy epitomizes a medical area where the interests of the sufferer and those of society may inevitably be in diametrical opposition. Paradoxically, the condition has been enshrined in English law before it has been effectively defined in medicine or psychiatry. It is characterized by persistently irresponsible or aggressive social behaviour. Needless to say psychopathic behaviour, which is always associated with emotional immaturity and poor socialization, is often encountered in the mentally subnormal. However, an appreciable proportion of psychopaths are of average or even superior intelligence. The condition is obstinate and constitutionally determined, accompanied in about one-third of all cases by EEG abnormalities, and shows no response to treatment, but often improves in some degree with the delayed emotional maturation that characterizes most of these patients. Despite well-intentioned judicial recommendations there is no evidence that formal psychiatric treatment is of any real help. There is no known consistent pathology, but the fairly large incidence of EEG abnormalities and the fact that violently psychopathic episodes are seen in a proportion of patients with temporal lobe epilepsy speak strongly for a constitutional rather than a psychopathological basis.

The inadequate psychopath either rubs along in a succession of casual occupations or joins the partially remitted schizophrenic as an habitué of the public parks. It is the violent aggressive psychopath who presents the real problem, and no society has found a solution to it. His behaviour is as likely to land him in prison as in hospital, depending on the circumstances of his offence, his social and educational status, and the nature of the facilities available. The term *psychopath* is administrative and legal rather than medical, and the problem is one for society as a whole and transcends the boundaries and the competence of medicine. Neither ordinary mental hospital care nor the presently overcrowded prison afford good conditions for the management of these cases. An indeterminate sentence is anathema to the law, but it is the only realistic way of dealing with the incorrigible psychopath, and it would best be served in a special institution, custodial rather than penal. These unhappy people are immune to punishment, and penal management is both immensely expensive and as doomed to failure as formal medical treatment. The only hope of coping with this immensely difficult problem is by the establishment of special institutions in which the patient can stay until his behaviour justifies a closely supervised trial outside. Such an institution must be much less than a prison and much more than a hospital. Its whole régime is involved, and such success as can be hoped for will also depend on social and medical after-care and support which at present is in desperately short supply. This is one of the most difficult problems that faces society and medicine, but it seems certain that new methods of management present the only hope of avoiding the wastage and misery of the present disorganized arrangements, the results of which are as capricious as they are expensive.

Human experimentation

It is chiefly amongst physicians and medical administrators that the socio-economic implications of new forms of treatment have aroused anxiety. The ethical problems raised by the increasing volume of research procedures that are undertaken on the other hand have predominently aroused the concern and sometimes the alarm of patients, and especially of patients' organizations, which are sometimes supported by physicians unconcerned for or positively antagonistic to research.

The ethical problems raised by clinical research relate mainly to new procedures, controlled therapeutic trials, and the general ethics of investigative medicine.

The difficulties of the therapeutic pioneer can be exaggerated. The surgeon who tries out a new operative procedure does so because he hopes for a better therapeutic result, and while events may prove him to have been unduly optimistic his good faith is rarely questioned. If the doctor who uses a new drug for the first time is satisfied that all possible steps have been taken to ensure that it is safe he has no real problem. On the other hand if the drug is really new, and the doctor is scientifically orientated as well as honest, he is quite likely to feel he should conduct a controlled therapeutic trial, in which the new treatment is measured against an established routine or, especially if there is no established routine treatment, against the effects of administering tablets of sugar or something similar. The ethics of the controlled trial have been much discussed. There are some distinguished British physicians who feel that while there is no need to warn the patient that he is being given a new drug in the ordinary course of clinical practice, it is dishonest to conduct a controlled trial without acquainting him that he is participating in it. The main reason for this objection is that it is regarded as introducing an element of deceit into the relationship between doctor and patient. I think most British physicians in fact ask the patient to collaborate in therapeutic experiments of this kind, but often omission of such information can hardly be regarded as of any particular importance. Because of variability in individual response the outcome of treatment in every patient is in the last resort uncertain. Every course of treatment is really an experimental trial, and other things being equal a controlled trial is likely to be more carefully supervised by a more scrupulous physician than the uncontrolled experiment of routine treatment. There is one real dilemma in this particular connection. For example, a very careful five-year clinical trial carried out concurrently in Newcastle and Edinburgh has indicated that the administration of Clofibrate (Atromid S) seems to have a remarkable effect on the prognosis of angina. This effect does not seem to improve the prospects of those who have had a cardiac infarcation without angina. The results look convincing and suggest something like a 50 per cent reduction in the expected number of further heart attacks during the period of observation. However, the history of the fiasco of routine anti-coagulant treatment, where tremendous resources were wasted and a good deal of harm done by treatment which we now know to be virtually worthless, renders it essential that these observations are carefully repeated elsewhere. The problem is quite simply how far it is ethical to ignore these favourable results by withholding Clofibrate from a further group of control patients. Of course if we were absolutely certain about the results of these two trials the withholding of the drug would be unethical. Some physicians already take this attitude at the present time and on the present evidence. However even the best designed and executed experiments may yield fallacious results, and most scientifically orientated physicians would consider it so important to get the answer right that further controlled trials are necessary to make absolutely certain. But here we approach another important ethical question: is it fair even possibly to disadvantage any individual patient with a view to adding to knowledge that will help others?

This problem arises very much more acutely in relation to investigation than in relation to treatment. Where the investigation is directly relevant to the patient's illness there can be no real problem except the professional measurement of the risks of the test against the dangers of the illness. But what about the critical area where investigations are undertaken not for the benefit of the patient himself, but to add to knowledge in the hope of helping future patients? A few doctors feel that this is never justified, but if it were abandoned medical advance would virtually cease. I think two conditions should always be met in this connection. First, the procedure should be carefully and honestly explained to the patient and his permission obtained. Secondly, the doctor himself should be convinced that the investigation is justified in that its probable contribution to medical knowledge outweighs the slight risk that is inseparable from almost any medical procedure.

One vexed question concerns the use of prisoners or mental defectives for mass experimentation. So far as can be discovered the several hundred mentally backward children at an American institution for the subnormal who have collaborated in valuable work on hepatitis which has led to advances that point the way to partial protection against this now dread disease were virtually conscripted, though parental consent was obtained. Observations carried out in Britain on the effects of intrathecal tuberculin injection under somewhat similar circumstances some years ago raised a storm of protest, and the hepatitis experiments have been criticized both in the United States and in Britain. The prison inmates who have taken part in medical experimentation and investigation have been volunteers, and on the face of it this seems unexceptionable. However, this procedure also has been castigated on the grounds that the prisoners would expect benefit of some kind for volunteering and were to that extent under some form of pressure. These issues deserve further discussion and consideration. They are not simple: after all, we inoculate millions of children against poliomyelitis so that a small number of them do not develop the disease. Despite a recognized risk of occasional serious complications, we vaccinate millions of people against smallpox, not so much for the benefit of each person vaccinated, but to protect society as a whole from the spread of the disease. When one considers the demands society makes from its members on very dubious moral grounds, especially in times of war, one sometimes feels that doctors are torturing themselves unnecessarily about such matters. Undoubtedly some over-enthusiastic human experimentation is ethically unjustifiable and frankly improper, but many morally motivated people regard all animal experimentation as immoral, even though we know that but for knowledge gained from animal experimentation some of the objectors would not be alive.

The population explosion

There are a number of causes for the rapid expansion of world population, but there can be no doubt first that this is due to reduced death-rates—especially in infancy—rather than to increased birth-rates, and secondly that the development of modern medicine has played and continues to play an extremely important part in this phenomenon. This field of study is confusing, and the student is caught in the cross-fire between the scientific harbingers of global doom and others, equally eminent, who regard the situation with relative complacency. It is a fair guess that the true situation lies somewhere between the two extremes.

All work in this field rests on the forward projection of present trends, with all its possible pitfalls. It is worth recalling that as recently as the 1920s distinguished statisticians and demographers were seriously concerned about a falling birth-rate, and predicted a gradual decline in the population of the United Kingdom. However, the real problem concerns world population and its uneven rate of growth in various parts of the world. There seems to be fairly general agreement that whatever can be achieved by long-term policies, nothing can now be done to prevent the world's population from doubling. Most of this increase is likely to occur in the underdeveloped countries. In India, Pakistan, and Indonesia almost half the present population is below the age of 15. History seems to show that when a society becomes wealthier and well-organized, its birth-rate falls and the rate of population expansion decreases, even though the contribution of medicine is likely to lead to a striking change in its age-distribution. The countries of western Europe are sometimes described as relatively stable in the matter of population—though there is a steady increase—and in some of the more rapidly developing countries such as Taiwan, Hong Kong, and Singapore there are already encouraging signs of decreasing fertility.

Nobody who has seen the slums of Calcutta or even the over-crowded squalor of the Indian countryside can doubt the reality of the problem of overpopulation, which continually baulks the country's effort to improve living standards. To the motorist who drives from Glasgow to Inverness the problem may seem less pressing, and there of course it is.

The problems of overpopulation affect the developing and the affluent countries quite differently. In the former, drought, flood, famine, starvation, and massive infection arise from the inability of the country to maintain food production and hygiene in a subsistence economy continually dragged down by the increasing numbers for which it has to cater. Unless population control can be achieved in these countries chaos seems to be merely a matter of time.

In the developed countries the problem is different and concerns first the enormous demands that each of us makes on the world's resources—especially of steel, oil, and protein; and secondly the vexed question of the quality of life. In this connection man's remarkable adaptability must be borne in mind. To any of the 200 000 inhabitants of Shakespeare's London the prospect of a conurbation of more than seven millions would surely have been unthinkable—and yet despite its many problems life in the metropolis today continues to attract many who could easily live and work in more salubrious and less uncomfortable conditions. On purely economic grounds a case could be made for moving the whole population of the British Isles to a built-up region south of Birmingham and using the rest of the United Kingdom as recreation space. Alternatively the rapid progress that is being made in new methods of food production make it imaginable for the whole surface of the British Isles to be populated as densely as London, with hundreds of millions of people sitting in their living capsules, feeding on soya-, yeast-, or algae-based protein and looking hopelessly for meaningful occupation. Food is probably not the limiting factor; the question is 'what kind of life?' It is the local differences that give life its flavour, and even in the richer countries the ordinary man feels an impotent resentment at the fact that the efforts of the planners to deal with a continually expanding urban population make all cities look increasingly like Birmingham or Cincinnati. In fact although the difficulties are undoubtedly more obtrusive in India or Japan, this is a world problem. Unchecked, the current growth rate of 2 per cent per annum would lead to a world population of 150 000 million in two centuries. In animal populations which cannot control their own fate, starvation, pestilence, and violence periodically and brutally adjust their overpopulation. Man has however the power to limit the birth-rate as well as to diminish death-rates, and there seems to be little doubt that in one form or another population control will become a necessary function of government. It is interesting that a lead in this connection has come from some of the more advanced countries of the Far East, including Japan and Taiwan.

Britain has an 0.8 per cent population growth annually, but this still means a very large increase of population within the present century, and if it were maintained it would double our present population in about 80 years. Even allowing for the development of new foodstuffs, ingenuity in rendering nuclear energy safe, and finding occupation for such a population, its material demands would be enormous and its contribution to pollution of the environment tremendous unless radical changes were effected in society. Quite apart from the difficult problem of nuclear waste disposal, there is good evidence that our phosphates would deoxygenate the ocean, and persistent pesticides and heavy metals in our environment would rise to truly dangerous levels.

Overpopulation is a world problem, but it almost certainly has to be dealt with on a national basis since the values of different countries and different societies vary widely. Two prevailing attitudes must be mentioned. Some developing countries resent being preached at about overpopulation, since they regard it as a sign of fear on the part of smaller and more affluent societies. This view is strengthened by the very inadequate efforts of most such affluent countries to deal with their own less frightening but still very real population problems. The fact is however that only the developed countries possess the technical expertise to develop, experiment with, and provide the methods of population control that must be made available to all.

How can we make progress in the United Kingdom and at the same time set an example and furnish help to other countries in this matter? The first thing is to make it easy to avoid the birth of unwanted children, such as most of the 80 000 illegitimate children born in Britain in 1970, and the 15 per cent of all legitimate births which are unwanted. The cost of a comprehensive family planning service including a domiciliary service furnished by health visitors chiefly for problem families might be as much as but not more than £60 millions a year. The cost of unwanted children in terms of public health and welfare resources is difficult to assess but the evidence suggests that the savings in supplementary benefits, child care facilities, medical treatment, and accommodation for the homeless would yield a ratio of benefit to cost of from 10 : 1 to 100 : 1 in different types of case. There can be no doubt that a comprehensive family planning service will be a national economy.

From a technical point of view there is every reason to anticipate improved contraception and simpler abortion, but it would be an immediate step forward to ensure now the easy availability and effective application of existing methods. Few general practitioners are willing to undertake contraceptive work, and far too few maternity hospitals offer it as an intrinsic part of their follow-up programmes. Family planning clinics are few and far between, and their clientele often consists chiefly of middle-class women rather than of those in greatest need, who in any case often require domiciliary service that is never available on the scale required. Needless to say, both contraception and abortion should be free. It is curious logic to demand payment for an effective procedure that is in the national interest while providing many other forms of treatment of questionable value to society, as well as to the individual, free of charge. A free and comprehensive family planning service would permit the exercise of choice in family size and reduce expenditure on social casualties as well as the rate of population growth.

It has been argued by some within the medical profession and outside it that a population policy is not only unjustified because of the uncertainty of predictive data, but would also be impracticable except within a framework of social compulsion incompatible with the freedom implicit in a democratic society. In relation to projected numbers the facts over the next two decades will speak for themselves. In relation to the second point it must be accepted that compulsory family limitation would certainly be unacceptable in the present climate. However, experience suggests that in the long term a combination of increasing wealth, intensive education, easily available professional assistance, and tax and other financial incentives might yield considerable dividends without compulsion.

4

Modern medicine and the third world

Deliberately, the discussion so far has concentrated on problems concerned with the application of scientific medicine in the affluent societies especially of western Europe and North America, where such issues as the care of the aged, the appropriate priority for transplant surgery, and the ethics of euthanasia are subjects of topical interest. If however we raise our eyes for a moment to problems of world health it immediately becomes evident that such an approach is introspective and even myopic. The most important dilemma in the world today—and the one most fraught with possibly appalling consequences for the future—arises from the enormous and increasing gulf between the developed and the undeveloped, the rich and poor countries of the world. This is the central issue of world politics. It is likely to dominate political thinking for the next half-century at least, and in this connection medicine is highly relevant.

Contemporary medical research is particularly concerned with the investigation of the subtle factors that underlie such intractable disease as multiple sclerosis, cancer of the breast, and hypertension. But looked at in a global context these are insignificant by comparison with the malnutrition, the persistence of infections and infestations that we have controlled in the affluent societies but which in Africa, Asia, and Latin America mean that half of all deaths occur in children under 5.

The export of modern scientific medicine to these countries was inevitable, and has been well-intentioned, but its results have not proved to be an unmixed blessing. It is cheap and relatively easy to send modern drugs round the world, and practicable to teach all but the most primitive populations methods of protection against infection by inoculation and vaccination provided the materials can be made available. But if the eradication of malaria or protection from tuberculosis merely means more mouths to feed in a country with high fertility and population growth, a subsistence agriculture, a capricious climate, and a primitive technology, its government's problems may be increased rather than diminished by the survival of many who would otherwise have died. Four hundred million people for example are still exposed to malarial infection, and more than 180 million are debilitated by bilharzia (schistosomiasis).

The governments of these countries face agonizing dilemmas. First, they must accept the awkward facts that the provision of piped water and mass vaccination programmes are more relevant to their situation than the sophisticated curative medicine that is the stock-in-trade of the orthodox western-style medical school. This situation is epitomized by the memory of an evening spent in Bombay when some very elegant electron microscope preparations were demonstrated in a room above a squalidly overcrowded hospital ward and overlooking a street in which people were sleeping huddled in every doorway and on every pavement. This impression has been strengthened by experience of clever and well-trained young Indian and Pakistani doctors coming to Britain, partly because they were unable to find appropriate employment in their own countries, to learn such techniques as haemodialysis and stereotaxic neurosurgery, sometimes returning home to find no opportunity to employ their skills except in a few small private hospitals, and more often than not ending up in Canada or Australia where their abilities are appreciated, employed, and adequately remunerated.

A few years ago my medical school was asked to advise one of the smaller African countries about the establishment of medical education in its university, and a series of meetings was held to discuss the problem. The visitors, who were for the most part politicians, expected to conjure up a medical school of international standard from the word go, although they had no idea either of the enormous expense involved or how appropriate students were to be found in a country with a pitifully low *per capita* income and a vestigial education system. Apparently collaboration in the venture with neighbouring countries was politically quite out of the question. Our suggestion that we would train a number of this country's students each year and build up a body of professionally skilled people while at the same time organizing a school in Africa for the training of medical auxiliaries was turned down flat, and the tone of the discussion was epitomized by their reply to a question on priorities; they had, so far as I remember, two surgeons, one physician, an anaesthetist, and a radiologist to serve the whole country, in addition to a handful of rural practitioners, and incredibly their top priority was for a forensic pathologist. This situation resolved itself when the whole delegation was arrested on its return home, and the negotiations were not resumed.

To return to Asia, the Indian predicament is characteristic and understandable. Unless the government trains a medical *corps d'élite* it will be unable to undertake the practical research into preventive medicine that is central to the Indian situation. Furthermore it will demoralize the medical profession to whom involvement in high technology is a matter of national pride, even if it is not always so easy to justify on utilitarian grounds. For reasons mentioned above they are bound to lose many of their best graduates to Europe and America, and of those who return most will join their colleagues in practice in the great cities. The problem of doctoring remote and scattered populations causes serious concern in countries as far apart as Canada and Siberia, to say nothing of Lancashire and northern Greece, but it is seen at its most desperate on the Indian subcontinent. Most of the doctors are of urban and middle-class origin and cannot face the cultural and financial deprivation inseparable from residence in a remote area amongst people with whom they often feel little in common. Fortunately bureaucrats can sometimes see further ahead than clinicians, and there are signs of a growing appreciation in many parts of the world that while the developing countries need to retain a foothold in scientific medicine their difficulties can be met only by developing new patterns of medical practice. In this connection the Chinese with their 'barefoot doctors' have led the way, and recently there are signs, for example, in India and Nigeria, of an increasing acceptance and the gradual establishment of a system based on simply trained medical workers who will sustain both an educative and public-health role, living within their communities, with access to expert professional advice and building a framework which can be gradually clothed with a clinical service. It is encouraging also that the provision of services always stimulates a demand for instruction in the techniques of family limitation.

A further problem is of course that the export of modern therapeutics to the third world has been unsupported by two other developments that would enhance its benefits and diminish its dangers: the simultaneous export of measures to control the population explosion, and of the knowledge and machinery to furnish an agricultural and industrial infrastructure without which it will never be able to sustain the heavy real cost of modern medicine. In the meantime millions of people all over the world die every year from diseases that can and could be controlled on the basis of existing knowledge and of techniques that are well within our grasp, if we had the will to apply them. The dangers implicit in the division between the rich and poor countries of the world pose a greater threat to the future of human civilization than the possibility of destruction by nuclear weapons, and it is important that the medical aspects of the situation should be fully realized. The important decisions to be taken are on the scale of world politics, but the contribution of medicine is essential: it could be central and immensely important.

Bibliography

BRITISH BROADCASTING CORPORATION (1970). *Morals and medicine. Five discussions from the BBC Third Programme* (ed. A. Clow). British Broadcasting Corporation, London.

COCHRANE, A. L. (1972). *Effectiveness and efficiency. Random reflections on health services.* (The Rock Carling Fellowship 1971). Nuffield Provincial Hospitals Trust, London.

COOPER, M. H. (1966). *Prices and profits in the pharmaceutical industry.* Pergamon Press, Oxford..

COUNCIL FOR INTERNATIONAL ORGANIZATIONS OF MEDICAL SCIENCES (CIOMS) (1970). *Medical research. Priorities and responsibilities. Proceedings of a round-table conference organized by CIOMS with the assistance of WHO and UNESCO: Geneva, 8–10 October 1969.* World Health Organization, Geneva.

CROSSMAN, R. H. S. (1972). *A politician's view of health service planning.* (Maurice Bloch lecture). University of Glasgow.

D'ARCY, P. F. and GRIFFIN, J. P. (1972). *Iatrogenic diseases.* Oxford University Press, London.

FEIN, R. and WEBER, G. I. (1971) *Financing medical education. An analysis of alternative policies and mechanisms.* McGraw Hill, New York.

KNOWLES, J. H. (ed). (1966). *The teaching hospital. Evolution and contemporary issues.* Harvard University Press, Cambridge, Massachusetts.

—— (ed). (1968). *Views of medical education and medical care.* Harvard University Press, Cambridge, Massachusetts.

KUNZE, R. M. and FEHR, H. (1972). *The challenge of life. Biomedical progress and human values.* Proceedings of the Roche 75th anniversary symposium held in Basel, Switzerland, 31 August to 3 September 1971 (Chairman: The Lord Todd, FRS). Birkhäuser Verlag, Basel and Stuttgart.

Bibliography

MEDICAL SERVICES REVIEW COMMITTEE (1962). *A review of the medical services in Great Britain* (Porritt Report). Social Assay, London.

NUFFIELD PROVINCIAL HOSPITALS TRUST (1968). *Screening in medical care. Reviewing the evidence. A collection of essays.* Oxford University Press, London.

—— (1970). *Problems and progress in medical care. Essays on current research. Fourth series* (ed. G. McLachlan). Oxford University Press, London.

—— (1971). *Challenges for change. Essays on the next decade in the national health service* (ed. G. McLachlan). Oxford University Press, London.

—— (1971). *Medical history and medical care. A symposium of perspectives* (arranged by the Nuffield Provincial Hospitals Trust and the Josiah Macy Jr Foundation) (ed. G. McLachlan and T. McKeown). Oxford University Press, London.

—— (1971). *Portfolio for health. The role and programme of the DHSS in health services research. Problems and progress in medical care. Essays on current research. Sixth series* (ed. G. McLachlan). Oxford University Press, London.

—— (1972). *Problems and progress in medical care. Essays on current research. Seventh series* (ed. G. McLachlan). Oxford University Press, London.

—— (1972). *Patient, doctor, society. A symposium of introspections* (ed. G. McLachlan). Oxford University Press, London.

OFFICE OF HEALTH ECONOMICS (1968). *Old age.* Office of Health Economics, London.

—— (1972). *Medical care in developing countries.* Office of Health Economics, London.

POYNTER, F. N. L. (ed). (1969). *Medicine and culture. Proceedings of a historical symposium organized jointly by the Wellcome Institute of the History of Medicine, London, and the Wenner-Gren Foundation for Anthropological Research, New York.* Wellcome Institute of the History of Medicine, London.

RUTSTEIN, D. D. (1967). *The coming revolution in medicine.* MIT Press, Cambridge, Massachusetts.

SOCIETY OF THE NEW YORK HOSPITAL (1972). *The future role of university-based metropolitan medical centers. Proceedings of the New York Hospital bicentennial colloquium.* Josiah Macy Jr Foundation, New York.

STEVENS, R. (1966). *Medical practice in modern England. The impact of specialization and state medicine.* Yale University Press, New Haven.

TAYLOR, G. RATTRAY (1968). *The biological time bomb.* Thames and Hudson, London.

WARTMAN, W. B. (1961). *Medical teaching in western civilization. A history prepared from the writings of ancient and modern authors.* Year Book Medical Publishers, Chicago.

Index